SPIRITUAL DETOX

Endorsements

'This very readable and uplifting book will encourage every Christian. Howard Satterthwaite, the current pastor of Westminster Chapel, and his wife Holly, have in their book *Spiritual Detox* touched a nerve in all of us who at times fall into discouragement. This book is so positive! There is not a person on the planet who has not needed a book like this. This timely and highly recommended book honours holy Scripture, the blood of Jesus and the Holy Spirit. I pray it will gain wide acceptance all over the world.'
Dr R.T. Kendall, senior minister of Westminster Chapel for twenty-five years, international speaker and bestselling author

'The challenge for any Christian teacher is to take God's eternal message and make it accessible to each new generation without changing the truth. In this book Howard and Holly Satterthwaite rise to the challenge and give us a fresh, insightful and utterly relevant treatment of the great biblical truths on confession and forgiveness. Here you will find depth of insight and height of vision, breadth of wisdom and sharpness of illustration, and a sense of God's holiness and of his grace.'
J. John, reverend canon

'Howard and Holly have a great track record of finding joy in tough places. Their words of wisdom and hope will help anybody who is looking for the joy that the Bible promises. Do yourself a favour and read this book!'
Phil Moore, leader of Everyday Church, London, writer of the *Straight to the Heart* series

'The most dangerous person in your church is the one who forgot he or she is a sinner. Or, as C.S. Lewis put it in *The Screwtape Letters*, "Indeed the safest road to Hell is the gradual one." The regular practice of confession of sin to God helps us to avoid the gradual road towards ignoring sin and its devilish effects. In this inspiring and helpful book, Howard and Holly Satterthwaite walk the reader through the why, the what and the

how of a life of confession before the Lord. Filled with biblical teaching and helpful application, and interspersed with stirring stories of believers set free through confession, this book is a must-read for any believer but especially for those who struggle with understanding how great is our God's grace and how full is his forgiveness.'
Ed Stetzer, Wheaton College

'I would encourage every believer to buy and devour this refreshingly honest book written by Howard and Holly. As more and more Christians in our day are crying out for revival, *Spiritual Detox* reminds us that repentance and confession are integral parts of God's alignment of his Church to his divine will. With powerful testimonies and clear teaching, this book challenges, encourages and equips. Read it, pray it and it will do your soul good.'
Guy Miller, leader of Commission.Global, an international movement of churches

'In a world obsessed with self-improvement and psychological well-being, this book will help you to see that only Christ can truly release us from the burdens of the past and the fears of the future. Its practical approach to confession as the God-given way to detox the soul is a truth that continues to change the lives of countless people.'
Justin Brierley, host of *Unbelievable?*, Premier Christian Radio

'Confession is a neglected but deeply liberating theme of the Christian faith, and one handled here with winning honesty, realism and joy. If we are to see more happy Christians and a renewal of the Church today, we need the message of this book.'
Dr Michael Reeves, president and professor of theology, Union School of Theology, Oxford, UK

'This book carries the same rawness and authenticity that Howard and Holly display in leading Westminster Chapel. An exciting read full of real-life stories about the power of confession and forgiveness. A very applicable and moving book serving as a reminder of the freedom that is available in Christ.'
Rachelle Ann Go, award-winning international musical theatre actress, star of *Hamilton* and *Les Misérables*

'Howard and Holly's warm pastoral hearts take us on a thoughtful, challenging, insightful and biblical journey on the vital place of confession and repentance in the life of the Christian. A timely reminder in days of much superficiality in the Church that how we begin the journey with Christ is how we are meant to continue! As the authors say: "Confession is not a journey of depressing introspection but life-transforming liberation – heavenly joy that transcends earthly circumstances." We are indeed redeemed to rejoice! I so enjoyed and was helped by this wonderful book.'
Trevor Archer, London director of the Fellowship of Independent Evangelical Churches

'God's ways work! They always have. They always will. In this joyful and accessible book, Howard and Holly unpack some of "God's ways" – his keys and principles for a free and healthy life. This book will do your heart good to read and even better to apply. Moreover, Howard and Holly are not theorists on this subject but practitioners. They have walked the road they are guiding us down. I encourage you to dive in and breathe the fresh air.'
Martin Storey, senior pastor, CLM Church, Coventry

'This is a timely book on an important, under-taught subject. It is biblically sound, theologically orthodox, contemporary, culturally connected and personally engaging. I highly recommend it.'
David Shearman, leader and founder of the Breakthrough Network of Churches and ecumenical canon in the Church of England

'This is a timely book. We live in a culture of individualism and self-centredness, which leaves us struggling to find meaning, identity and healthy relationships. In such a time confession truly is a liberating spiritual detox. It takes us back to where we belong, relating to ourselves, to God and to others in a real way. With refreshing honesty and culturally relevant perspectives, Howard and Holly inspire and guide us to the path of ongoing forgiveness. Enjoy the stories of real people who have experienced the power of confession along with practical tools to relate to the spiritual truths. A well-thought-through, balanced book obviously driven by the passion of Howard and Holly to see people experience freedom and a joyful life.'
Lars Due-Christensen, founder of STEPS, senior leader at Christ Church London

'*Spiritual Detox* is a refreshing and helpful guide, full of important information for anyone who yearns to go deeper into fellowship with God. Two pieces of advice: be warned, you may shed many tears as I did whilst reading it. Also, be prepared to experience the freedom and ecstasy that come from incorporating the discipline of confession as the ultimate lifestyle change. It works and it's more effective than diet and exercise. On top of that, it's free and has absolutely no bad side effects.'
Amicky Carol Akiwumi, MBE

'I can't think of a question that we struggle with more than telling the truth to and about ourselves. Even Christians, who confess a gospel of repentance and redemption, can struggle with the most basic discipline of confession. In *Spiritual Detox*, the Satterthwaites remind us that the way forward isn't through guilt or shame but through the grace and welcome of God, a grace and welcome that invites us into the truth. About ourselves, our actions, and our need of him.'
Hannah Anderson, award-winning author of *All That's Good: Recovering the Lost Art of Discernment*

'With fresh insight on a familiar concept, Howard and Holly Satterthwaite's *Spiritual Detox* is filled with biblical knowledge and human experience, reminding us of the nature of sin whilst highlighting God's ever-forgiving character. This book brings deeper insight into the importance of confession, showing us how the act of repentance can lead to spiritual freedom and open the doors for a deeper understanding of God's abounding grace and love for us all.'
Tope Koleoso, senior pastor, Jubilee Church London

'When we hear the word *confession*, our response is bad memories, guilt or even spiritual abuse. Howard and Holly Satterthwaite help us see confession for what it really offers: liberation and joy. They write, "Confession is the key that opens the door to celebratory joy." In this wide-ranging treatment, they reach all of us: those who are tired of faux apologies like "I'm sorry you were offended," those who run from guilt with "don't care" or "despair" and those who think about confession but never practice it. Howard and Holly not only share vulnerably from their own lives, they also offer us a path to joy through confession, even providing wonderful prayers for us to use. I have known Howard and Holly for some years.

They are brilliant, big-hearted and unpretentious. Their leadership at Westminster Chapel is remarkable. I am thrilled that more of us will discover their needed voice in this excellent book.'
Steve Cuss, author of *Managing Leadership Anxiety: Yours and Theirs*

'A disclaimer for our endorsement of *Spiritual Detox*: we love Howard and Holly. They are some of the most humble, intelligent, transparent leaders in the Church today. That being said, *Spiritual Detox* is a beautifully written, immensely readable treatment of the often-overlooked value of confession in the spiritual life of a Christ follower. Even if we didn't know and love the Satterthwaites we would highly recommend this book to anyone looking to grow in their faith. Because we do know and love them, we can't recommend their book enough.'
Geoff Surratt, CEO, Ministry Together and **Sherry Surratt,** geographic vice president, One Hope

'*Spiritual Detox* is one of those books that you don't want to put down, not only for its content but for its creative writing. This book masterfully and beautifully narrates the story of man and the heart of God. *Spiritual Detox* offers guidelines for the present day studded with life-changing testimonies and helpful questions, and is simply a blessing to read. If anyone desires freedom from the bondage of sin and a closer walk with God, then read *Spiritual Detox* and allow yourself to embrace the powerful spiritual truths set forth.'
Vinu Paul, apostolic leader, responsible for Commission.Global churches in South East Asia and leader of Living Hope Church, Mumbai, India

'If your soul is dry, if joy is a distant memory, if you know what you are in public is not what you are in private, this book is for you. With disarming honesty, Howard and Holly Satterthwaite invite us to lay down our hiding, blame-shifting and justifications and bring our sins to the all-sufficient cross of Jesus. The truth in this book offers more than a detox of the soul but a renewal of our life in Christ.'
Tim Rudge, field director, UCCF: The Christian Unions

SPIRITUAL DETOX

Discovering the Joy of
Liberating Confession

By Howard Satterthwaite
With
Holly Satterthwaite

FORM

First published in Great Britain in 2021

Society for Promoting Christian Knowledge
36 Causton Street
London SW1P 4ST
www.spck.org.uk

British Library Cataloguing-in-Publication Data
A catalogue record for this book is available from the British Library

ISBN 978-0-281-08627-6
eBook ISBN 978-0-281-08628-3

1 3 5 7 9 10 8 6 4 2

Typeset by Westchester Publishing Services
Printed and bound in the UK by Jellyfish Print Solutions

eBook by Westchester Publishing Services

Produced on paper from sustainable forests

To

Anna and Isaac – may you ever increasingly
know the God of extraordinary joy.

Contents

Foreword

This is an important and timely book.

The subject of confession may feel like a challenging one. In a permissive society where 'anything goes', reflecting on our less pleasant thoughts, feelings and behaviours can feel countercultural. For some Christians, this sometimes-neglected practice may be associated with bad memories of guilt or shame. For others, even those who do not have these negative associations, the discipline of confession can be hard to maintain.

This could not be further from the picture painted in this book. Howard and Holly's insights breathe fresh life into this subject. This book is so positive! The joy and the welcome of God that they have both experienced through the incorporation of confession into their daily devotional lives jumps out of the pages. Far from being about guilt or shame, or even the mundanity of ritualistic practice, this book reminds us that confession is life-giving, bringing liberation and freedom in our spiritual lives.

On the day this manuscript arrived, I, Debby, was hurting from the way in which a friend had behaved towards me. This was not the first time. I had forgiven many times before, and this time I was considering drawing a line. I felt I was done! Then I saw it – *Discovering the Joy of Liberating Confession* – a book about confession, repentance and forgiveness, and I sensed that the Lord was speaking. As I read the first chapters I was melted. Tears came to my eyes as I poured out my heart to God. I repented of nearly giving up and potentially retaliating with rejection and silence. I forgave and I felt the hurt lift and love return. Honestly, it was so freeing.

Howard and Holly are the real deal. Holly was part of our church while she was a student, and their faith and passion for God and desire for others to know him better are reflected in the joyous way confession is written about in this book. They have such pastoral hearts, and this book takes the reader on a gentle and loving journey into understanding how confession can help us to experience the extravagant grace of God, leading us into a deeper experience of his presence and fellowship with us.

It is no mean feat to make ancient truths so accessible to a new generation without changing those truths. Howard and Holly have risen to the challenge. This book is underpinned by biblical insights and deep theological understanding, shared in a fresh and engaging package. The way they have laid out confession, repentance and both giving and receiving forgiveness is clear and easy to understand. They make the subject accessible, and we believe this will bring significant healing to spiritual sickness in the lives of believers and unbelievers alike.

But this is not a theory textbook. There are practical suggestions and examples. Howard and Holly share their own experiences and real-life stories. Many will be able to relate to the examples given. Their vulnerability and modelling of spiritual leadership are clear to see.

Leaning into confession, repentance and forgiveness can renew and deepen our spiritual lives and draw us closer to the Lord in such exciting ways. Moreover, as we hope for renewal in the Church and revival in our land, this book will make a significant contribution in paving the way.

We have been so blessed by Howard and Holly's obedience in writing this insightful book, and we wish you every blessing as you engage with its pages.

John and Debby Wright, national directors, Vineyard Churches, UK & Ireland

Introduction

'In a world where everything has gone so sadly astray, we should be standing out as men and women apart, people characterised by a fundamental *joy* . . .'

Dr Martyn Lloyd-Jones, *Spiritual Depression*

Have you ever eaten too much? It happens to me, especially at Christmas. I feel fat, uncomfortable and lethargic. Oh, and let's not forget bloated: Brussels sprouts, aka gas grenades, hatch their plans against me (and my immediate neighbours).

Worse – can it get any, after that sentence? – I become irritable as well. Grumpy that I can't have my Christmas dinner, pudding, cake and eat it. Why shouldn't I be able to stuff my face while feeling like an energetic twenty-something with a six-pack? Doesn't culture tell us that we're entitled to have everything and anything we want? This slothful stupor we can feel physically happens to us spiritually too when we put ourselves first.

If we greedily let our unbridled appetites win out – be they selfish ambitions or an insatiable search for approval, that desperate need to be liked no matter what – we can quickly find ourselves reduced to the role of spiritual couch potato, so consumed with sinful distractions and overwhelmed at the prospect of changing ourselves that we can lose zeal and faith for the life and purpose God has called us to. In short, when we major on sin and minor on confession, we become full of that most toxic and inescapable of dead weights – the mysterious thing we call guilt.

We see two types of guilt: 'big G' Guilt, and for now let's call it 'little g' guilt. The latter is the negative feeling we get for, say, not living up to a family or cultural expectation. That doesn't need confession.

You can fight it by knowing what you should feel Guilty about, with a big 'G'. That's your conscience telling you you've broken one of God's universal laws, which does require confession. If you zoom out, you'll see a world wrestling with guilt. The guilt of entrenched sexism (#metoo) and overt and structural racism (#blacklivesmatter), alongside our environmental sins (#gretathunberg, #extinctionrebellion) and global injustices (#sweatshops, #unfairtrade). People are coming to terms with the fact that we are not just part of the cure but the disease. Guilt is engulfing us at every level.

Oh, and guilt (feeling rotten) has a friend: shame (feeling dirty). They're sort of best friends, actually, so much so that it's often hard to know where one begins and the other ends. 'Shame,' psychologist and theologian Edward T. Welch says, 'is the deep sense that you are unacceptable because of something you did, something done to you, or something associated with you. You feel exposed and humiliated. Or, to strengthen the language, you are disgraced because you acted less than human, you were treated as if you were less than human, or you were associated with something less than human, and there are witnesses.'[1] We're focusing on the 'something you did . . . acted less than human' part in this book. But we should point out that although we can experience shame without personally sinning – by being a victim of another's sin, for example – we often react sinfully in response to the shame of being sinned against, which brings on the guilt. They really are joined at birth. The 'I *am* wrong' of shame, sourced in the 'I've done wrong' of guilt, cuts deep.

The consequence? Our inner life can become a joyless wasteland. We busily fill our lives to steer clear of that void, to stop ourselves from being confronted with the desert places that exist in our minds and hearts.[2] Yet when the world around us quietens down, we know that something inside us isn't right. But what can we do about it? Society's dictating drumbeat of 'the show must go on' never seems to stop playing.

So we hide from God,[3] ourselves and others . . . and become as inauthentic as the surrounding culture, a culture that's all about faking it. Which leads us to an interesting British newspaper headline: 'People Call Me an Oompa Loompa.'[4] It's the story of a tanorexic woman who has spent £30,000 maintaining her fake orange glow over the years. We may laugh at her, but are we really so different? We edit images, only posting the near-perfect parts of our lives on social media. We become part and parcel of the fake society we live in: fake handbags, fake news, even fake music bands (google 'Threatin').

Do you also share our longing for authenticity, to embrace a deeper sense of reality?[5] We believe that you, like us, want freedom from having to fake it. You don't want to live in denial. You don't want to be *spiritually* fat, lethargic and irritable. You want to face the music and dance, to confess with honest vulnerability and be set free to live in loving forgiveness. You want to detox all that bad stuff we call sin that accumulates, entangles and suffocates your soul, taking away your joy.

Yes, joy! That is fundamentally what this book is about. The greatest feel-good factor in the world, which comes from knowing you're forgiven by the greatest being in the world – granting 'joy that is inexpressible and filled with glory' (1 Pet. 1.8). Confession is not a journey of depressing introspection but life-transforming liberation – heavenly joy that transcends earthly circumstances. If we see it as an unpleasant duty rather than an invitation to freedom, we'll struggle to make it a regular part of our daily lives. You'll miss out and maybe even take some depressing wrong turns, exhaustingly trying to win favour with God and experience him close again by, for example, *religiously* obsessing over your 'quiet times' with God. This is why we must discover (again) the what, why, when, how of confession – develop our understanding of it to empower us to do it.

Confession is the ultimate detox, a gazillion times more powerful than my routine intake of Sweet Himalayan Detox Green Tea (this is Howard, by the way – assume 'I' and 'me' are always Howard unless we tell you otherwise). No earthly detox can reach the part of you only God can touch. Confession is the ultimate detox because it's a soul detox, and the soul, to quote spiritual philosopher Dallas Willard, is 'the inner stream which refreshes, nourishes and gives strength to every other element of our life'.[6] If your soul is dammed up with guilt, everything else dries up. To mix metaphors, guilt has a stranglehold on the soul, starving you of the oxygen of joy.

It's a persistent problem. American intellectual historian Wilfred M. McClay says: 'Guilt has not merely lingered. It has grown, even metastasised, into an ever more powerful and pervasive element in the life of the contemporary West, even as the rich language formerly used to define it has withered and faded from discourse . . .'[7] Attempts to avoid it or box it away as a subjective emotion are like trying to hold down an inflatable beach ball under the sea; it will inevitably come back up to the surface.

This is because guilt isn't just a cultural or religious construct. It's more like the certain hurt we feel if we foolishly attempt to defy gravity. As Martin Luther King Jr said in 1954, 'reality hinges on moral foundations', and 'there are moral laws of the universe just as abiding as the physical laws . . . And so we just don't jump out of airplanes or jump off high buildings for the fun of it . . . Because we unconsciously know that there is a final law of gravitation, and if you disobey it you suffer the consequences.'[8]

Jordan Belfort, the real 'Wolf of Wall Street', played by Leonardo DiCaprio in the movie of the same name, is one who did 'suffer the consequences'. He greedily cheated people out of millions of dollars so he could live a luxurious lifestyle of debauched 1990s excess. Did he find joy? No! Today he says, 'I lost my *soul* as much as a person can and still be walking around.'[9] You can't escape guilt for breaking God's universal laws of morality, or, to use the biblical language, for sinning. You can ignore, deny or justify guilt, or project it onto others, but it remains present, even through your very refusal to accept it.

But who says these universal laws have to be God's? Good question; permit us to answer it with another: where do you think the curious idea that we ought to behave in a certain way comes from?[10]

Some atheists, like Michael Ruse, have argued that morality is just 'a biological adaptation',[11] asserting it evolved from genetic programming to care for those who share your genes and scratch the backs of those who scratch yours. But this selfish me-me-me code of conduct isn't much of a morality; it could even be immorality. It cannot account for random acts of kindness and Good Samaritan behaviour. Plus, it's deterministic, suggesting you're only 'good' because you're programmed to be that way. Oh, and don't forget it's not absolute. It changes according to majority rule, which means you can't make 'true for everyone, everywhere' statements like 'rape is evil' unless, and this is important to note, *unless* you're living above or inconsistently with your worldview, i.e., borrowing from Christianity.[12]

You – we – need confession because we all have a guilt problem. It's not something the Church made up to control you (although we admit it's definitely been abused and we are so sorry if you're one of the Church's victims). Guilt is real. To dismiss guilt as a cultural or religious construct is to tell people that their past sin and wrongdoing don't matter. Which means the people they've sinned against and the hurt, pain and suffering they've caused don't matter either. That's a problem. It also means that the hurt, pain and suffering caused by others to you and those you love don't matter. If a drunk driver killed your child, would you say it doesn't matter? We don't think you would.

Guilt is real and it's a real joy-killer. It's more crushing and even crippling than we realise. A respected medical sociologist, Hans Kellner, was once presented with a woman with a paralysed arm.[13] Nothing brought any improvement whatsoever, so they tried psychotherapy. Eventually, a deep wound in her life emerged. She'd used this previously sound arm to destroy the life growing in her womb. The guilt was so intense she unconsciously punished herself by paralysing the arm that had performed the act. Guilt haunted her. She reminds me of a former inmate, convicted of manslaughter in the States, whom I interviewed when interning at a death penalty defence law firm. He said, 'Nothing I do can ever erase the painful memory of the harm I've caused; I still see the man I killed every day when I look at myself in the mirror.'

Guilt is more than just a burden you carry on your back; it's poison in your soul. It can make you depressed, and even crazy if you don't deal with it rightly. Kurt Cobain, frontman of the flagship band of Generation X, Nirvana, cited 'feeling guilty beyond words' in his suicide note.[14] Could guilt be contributing, *at least in part*, to our current 'mental health crisis'?[15] In short: yes, but. Sin can be a wrongly overdiagnosed cause in mental illness, especially by some in the Church. We should not jump to conclusions, so as to avoid false guilt. Mental health struggles can be the result of losing things essential to our humanity, like meaningful interaction with others, not simply sin. But it can also be a wrongly underdiagnosed cause, especially in secular societies. The head of a large English psychiatric facility is reported to have said, 'I could dismiss half my patients tomorrow if they could be assured of forgiveness.'[16]

Like Pontius Pilate in the crucifixion narrative, we all want to find a way to wash our hands clean, because, truth be told, we're all guilty. We've all done wrong, whether in something we said, did or failed to do; we've all told lies to protect ourselves; we've all selfishly hurt others in the pursuit of our own agendas – and that's just the things we're aware of. Millions of microbes exist all around us beyond view. But when you put a microscope to them, a whole world of 'beasties' suddenly comes into sight. Under God's eyes, how many more sicknesses of the soul are there visible to him that we never see ourselves? Too many. But this needn't haunt us. We needn't lose our minds to 'life's fitful fever'[17] like Shakespeare's Lady Macbeth, trying day after day to wash the invisible blood from her guilty hands. Why? Because through confession we can find the joy of forgiveness.

Something I desperately needed

More on that shortly, but right now you might be wondering what led us to write a book on confession. Well, it started in a pastoral care session I had with a precious member of our church. I found myself speaking about the certain hope of forgiveness available through confession. I slowly read these first-century words inspired by God, written by John – 1 John 1.9, the verse this book is all about:

> If we confess our sins, he is faithful and just to forgive us our
> sins and cleanse us from all unrighteousness.

After a few more words of encouragement, the fellow leader and trusted friend[18] pastoring with me said, 'That one verse could be an entire preaching series on a subject that's desperately needed in the Church today.' Boom! At that moment a divine download happened. I saw 1 John 1.9 broken up in my mind, and in the weeks that followed God helped me to put flesh on that skeleton, and almost a year later we preached the series. But what began as a series for the church was also something I desperately needed.

As I progressed in my walk with God, I was becoming more and more aware of my sin. This intensified to something of a breaking point under the increasing pressures of church leadership. Most prominent was ungodly ambition. When I was appointed lead pastor of Westminster Chapel, there were some surprised and even dissenting voices. I wanted to prove them wrong. I wanted praise for being the one to get the church firing on all cylinders, going boldly where others had not gone before. I wanted to silence critics who thought I wasn't theologically mature enough, so I liked the idea of going one better than world-respected preacher and former minister at the chapel, Mr 'Logic-on-Fire', Dr Martyn Lloyd-Jones. In his seventy-seven-sermon series on 1 John, this amazing man, to the best of my knowledge, did not preach a specific message on the verse

God had drawn to our attention. We were going to do nine! Finally, I thought, I might not be completely obliterated by the shadow of this man's greatness.[19]

This was hideous pride and horrible envy, stemming from insecurity, and guilt's toxicity was taking its toll. I had become driven by tunnel vision of a worldly definition of success. I'd become anxious about attendance numbers and fearful about the future, the possibility of losing my job and relocating my family if I failed to deliver growth. I was becoming distant from God, struggling to abide in the beloved child identity he generously bestows on us who believe.

So I soaked in 1 John 1.9. I meditated upon it and studied it in great detail in preparing to preach the series mentioned, and it stayed with me. I started to journal daily confessions of sin in my prayer times, and I began to change. Sure, I did a few other things that helped, like check in with a good Christian counsellor, but confession played a vital part. In looking down at the depths of my sin, I was able to look up at the sweet mercy of God and see just how far he had come to forgive and cleanse me from it. Going deep, like sinking down on a trampoline, enabled me to bounce high with joy, marvelling at the amazing grace of God. I am far from the finished article. I continue to wrestle with my sin. For example, I didn't initially want to write this book with my wife, Holly. I wanted any glory for myself, even though I knew her involvement would make it a better book. Yikes! But through confession, through trying to live what I am teaching, I am making progress. Pray for me.

During this time, we also started to talk with church leaders and friends from different denominations and movements, as well as our own, about confession. We conducted a small survey, which confirmed our suspicions that confession is a seriously neglected discipline in the lives of church leaders and attenders and in Sunday services. We only came across one book specifically on confession.[20] Other books on the spiritual disciplines made little mention of this foundational practice and/or cast it primarily as confessing to, or in

8

the presence of, another believer. There are different reasons for this. For example, confession is seen as a formal thing Roman Catholics are required to do, which our tribe of twenty-first-century Protestants can all too easily, and perhaps reactively, ignore. But we do so at our peril. Now, please don't misunderstand us, we are not advocating constructing confessionals. We are arguing for liberating confession, setting it free from exile and error, restoring it to restore joy.

The 'capital C' Church today is a bit like Austin Powers without his mojo – only we're talking about the irresistible attraction of divine joy, of course, not sexual magnetism. We are not that different from the faltering institutions and failing leaders of our society. We need to get our mojo joy back. Dr Martyn Lloyd-Jones put it far more eloquently in *Spiritual Depression*: 'In a world where everything has gone so sadly astray, we should be standing out as men and women apart, people characterised by a fundamental *joy*'. But, he continues, 'You must be made miserable before you can know true Christian joy.'[21]

That's why we need Jesus, the Great Physician's medicine of confession.[22] It's like disinfecting a wound: the treatment stings for a short time, so it can heal for the long haul.

Redeeming to rejoice

Recovering joy is one of three key reasons we must liberate confession. It's about dusting off and cleaning up an ancient daily practice. A bestselling Christian author wrote: 'Many followers of Christ experience a moment of grace, but not a lifetime of grace. They go through life under a cloud not really enjoying grace even though they've heard loads about it. What is missing is an indispensable tool for a healthy and authentic spiritual life . . . a practice that spiritually wise people have known about for centuries. What we need in the church today is more followers of Christ who really know how to confess.'[23]

Confession is about getting rid of guilt and every trace of related shame, to walk more closely with the God of joy who sings love songs over his children. That's the context of 1 John 1.9. Verse 3 of chapter 1 speaks of an invitation to enjoy the same close, intimate fellowship of holy love the apostle John had with Jesus, complemented by verse 6, which refers again to 'fellowship with him', God the Father, Son and Holy Spirit. So why is John, first-century apprentice to Jesus, writing this letter to Christians[24] about fellowship (something you can lose, and become spiritually depressed about, unlike salvation)?

Verse 4 says 'to make our [and your] joy complete'. Both translations are legitimate: John is writing to perfect individual *and* corporate joy (which flow into and out of each other). In Pss. 32 and 51 we meet David, the king whose adultery begat murder. He'd lost his mojo joy. 'For when I kept silent about my sin,' he says, 'my bones wasted away . . . [and] my strength was dried up.'[25] In Ps. 51 he confesses his sin to recover what? Joy! 'Let me hear *joy* and gladness . . . let the bones you have crushed *rejoice* . . . Restore to me the *joy* of your salvation . . .'[26]

When the wild-living son in Jesus' famous prodigal parable[27] comes to his senses and returns, he doesn't take on the status of a forgiven slave but a beloved son. He is forgiven. His pig muck, guilt and shame are covered by the Father's embrace, swallowed up by the gifts of robe, ring and sandals, and lost in happy festivities.

Confession is the key that opens the door to this celebratory joy. But sometimes it's hard to understand what that joy feels and looks like, isn't it? So, to whet your appetite, think of Andy Dufresne, played by Tim Robbins, in *The Shawshank Redemption*. It's the moment in this top-rated movie that Andy finally breaks free after nineteen years of incarceration, crawling out of a narrow sewage pipe – he rips off his prison clothes, strides forward and looks heavenward. It's a picture of the triumph of liberating joy that can be yours through confession. Watch the clip if you have time,[28] or, better still, read the true stories of forgiveness (from people, past and present, connected to Westminster Chapel)[29] at the start of each chapter. May they teach you to treasure confession as you deepen your own experience of forgiveness.

Slowing down to savour

The second reason we need confession is that we live in an age of dangerous digital distraction that wants to keep us superficially busy doing what it wants, which isn't confession, and that isn't good.

The former Facebook president Sean Parker said:

> The thought process that went into building these applications, Facebook being the first of them . . . was all about: 'How do we consume as much of your time and conscious attention as possible?' And that means that we need to sort of give you a little dopamine hit every once in a while, because someone liked or commented on a photo or a post or whatever. And that's going to get you to contribute more content, and that's going to get you . . . more likes and comments. It's a social-validation feedback loop . . . exactly the kind of thing that a hacker like myself would come up with, because you're exploiting a vulnerability in human psychology.[30]

There are forces out there working hard to keep you hurrying on their hamster wheel, getting you to think, act, consume and vote for what they want. They want to keep you busy coveting and comparing, distracting you from savouring and serving Jesus, bombarding you with an overwhelming 5,000 adverts a day.[31] They don't want you to have the time to stop and think about what really matters: your soul and its need for forgiveness and fellowship with Jesus.

Confession is an act of defiance against digital distraction. It's a daily invitation to shut out its noise. It's an appeal to slow down. To stop waterskiing superficially over guilt and scuba dive deep into the ugliness of sin, but only for a short time, so that you can even more slowly savour and feast upon the forgiveness of God.

Renewing to revive

The final reason for recovering confession is to open the door to revival. Yes, we know that is a bold statement, but we believe it is justified. Writing about sixteenth- and seventeenth-century Pietism and Puritanism, Professor Richard Lovelace said: 'Reforming doctrines and institutions in the church was futile [in bringing about revival] unless people's lives were reformed and revitalised.'[32] Jonathan Edwards, also known as America's greatest theologian, said the revivals in the eighteenth century that he experienced broke out from a true awareness of sin. The taverns (pubs) were no longer popular as people flocked to pastors' homes instead. The first point of Evan Roberts' four-point message – which seemed to fan into flame the 1904–5 Welsh Revival, resulting in 70,000 people trusting in Jesus in the first two months – was 'Confess any known sin to God.'[33] Confession is essential to personal, inner, heart transformation. Like the proverbial stone dropped in a lake, it can cause ripple effects, concentric circles of renewal spreading from person to person, laying the foundation for corporate revival.

Canon Max Warren in his enquiry on revival wrote: 'One of the dominant impulses from which revival is born is a recovered awareness of the exceeding sinfulness of sin.' That awareness is how confession begins but thankfully not how it ends. Confession is the detox we need to fully delight in Christ – if, and it's a big if, we accept Jesus' invitation (through John) to do it. That is the subject of the next chapter.

But before getting into that, at the end of each chapter we have included some questions for you to pause and reflect upon, and a written confession from the Bible or the pen of a church leader, from the first century to today. We have intentionally collated these prayers to support you in cultivating a regular rhythm of confession and repentance. The goal of this book is not for you merely to know more about confession but to inspire you to do more confessing. We want confession to bless your life the way it has ours and the lives of *so* many others. These prayers provide a helpful structure for confession times with God, especially when we feel tongue-tied or uncertain how to pray. Read them aloud and meditate on them in your heart. Better still, rewrite them in your own words. Please make time to learn more about confession by practising it as you progress through this book.

Questions for reflection

What did you think about confession before you read this chapter?

Why is biblical confession *the* detox people need?

What difference could daily confession make to your life, church, neighbourhood?

Prayer of Confession
Have mercy on me, O God,
according to your steadfast love;
according to your abundant mercy
blot out my transgressions.
Wash me thoroughly from my iniquity,
and cleanse me from my sin!

For I know my transgressions,
and my sin is ever before me.
Against you, you only, have I sinned
and done what is evil in your sight,
so that you may be justified in your words
and blameless in your judgement.
Behold, I was brought forth in iniquity,
and in sin did my mother conceive me.
Behold, you delight in truth in the inward being,
and you teach me wisdom in the secret heart.

Purge me with hyssop, and I shall be clean;
wash me, and I shall be whiter than snow.

Questions for reflection

Let me hear joy and gladness;
let the bones that you have broken rejoice.
Hide your face from my sins,
and blot out all my iniquities.
Create in me a clean heart, O God,
and renew a right spirit within me.
Cast me not away from your presence,
and take not your Holy Spirit from me.
Restore to me the joy of your salvation,
and uphold me with a willing spirit.
Ps. 51.1–12

Forgiveness story #1

CRAIG

I was serving at Her Majesty's pleasure for drug-induced breaking and entering and a firearms offence. I was angry and ashamed. Sure, I could blame the tough upbringing I'd had, but I knew that was just an explanation, not an excuse. I was primarily responsible for the hurt and pain for which I was rightly being punished. I felt like I had this massive weight on my back. There was this terrible sense of hopelessness I was trying to hide from. Guilt was eating me up inside.

I knew God existed, but I didn't know who he was. I didn't think he'd want to forgive me anyway. I'd have to earn it and I couldn't because, well, look at me, a criminal – I'd blown it. One day I was desperate enough to try going to a church service. A guy was speaking who had a similar story to mine. He was a drug dealer who'd been in and out of prison until he met Jesus. He started to go through the Bible, referencing person after person God had forgiven. '*If* God can forgive David for adultery and murder, and *if* God can forgive Paul for killing believers, why do you think he can't forgive you?' His question resonated deeply with me. It was as if a door had been opened and the light was beginning to shine through it, helping me to see that it might just be possible, with my not-so-dissimilar story, that I could be forgiven.

As I began to read the Bible for myself and attend Bible studies led by real Christians, my eyes were opened fully to see how forgiveness is possible through the death and resurrection of Jesus Christ. When I said a prayer of confession and repentance for the first time, I sensed a great burden of unforgiveness lift off me and a deep inner peace and spirit of well-being took up residence inside. I'd finally found what I'd been looking for. I was still in prison but I was free.

In the months since that day, I've grown in my understanding of God's generous forgiveness through regular confession. I'm getting better at going to God straight away. Initially, I felt like I had to punish myself when I sinned – the 'you have to earn this' mindset was lodged deep in my psyche. I'd self-isolate and mentally beat myself up, sometimes for a few hours, sometimes even for days, only going to God when I thought I'd done enough. Now I realise I'm doing Jesus a disservice by acting like that. He paid it all at the cross. There's nothing I can add to his perfect work of salvation.

God is a good Father and he is faithful to forgive. He sorts me out when I soil myself with sin and sends me out again and again, every time I fall, to serve him. I don't wallow in that miry pit of unforgiveness any more.

1

If

'Better, though difficult, the right way to go,
Than wrong, though easy, where the end is woe.'
John Bunyan, *The Pilgrim's Progress*

If is a short but very significant word. In 1 John 1.9 it is both a choice and a promise. Yes, this book is about helping you develop the joy-giving *practice* of confession. But to do that we must first refresh our *understanding*, beginning with the basics: confession is a choice and a promise.

The choice

Every day we make hundreds of choices from the mundane to the monumental. Some sources suggest the average person makes 35,000 choices per day.[1] If correct, that's 2,000 every hour! Some of these choices are hard and some are easy. Let me talk you through my biannual challenge when I visit the opticians for an eye test.[2] They sit me down, tell me to look at the chart at the end of the room, cover one of my eyes and put different lenses in front of the other. Then they ask, 'Is it clearer with this one or this one? With number one or number two?' But I'm thinking, 'I don't know! They look the same. Is this a trick question? Help! What if I end up with the wrong prescription?'

The choice to confess or not confess is not meant to be hard in that sense. It's meant to be obviously good for you, like giving up smoking, cutting out junk food and going to the gym. They are all blatantly beneficial for your well-being. That's why millions of us make resolutions to do them at the start of each new year. But as we all know, those resolutions rarely last. The 55-million-user app Strava, from their extensive research of fitness resolutions, say the day we're most likely to quit is 19 January[3] – which interestingly seems to correlate with Blue Monday (the most depressing day of the year, apparently). So much for will power. We figure the present pain outweighs the gain, so we give up. The easy choice turns out to be a lot harder than we thought.

That's how you could feel about confession, if you put it in the same earthly category, despite it being of a higher order, promising a gain that is infinitely greater than looking good at the beach on holiday. Confession's reward makes all the other prizes look like wooden spoons.

What's extraordinary is that God isn't asking you to do penance, to sweat on a treadmill for hours, to obtain it. No, we're just talking about a few words said with full understanding from the heart. OK, we admit that last part is a bit difficult – and painful, like surgery – because it means you have to face your true self to find freedom. John Bunyan gives imaginative voice to this in *Pilgrim's Progress*, one of the bestselling books in the world:

> This hill, though high, I covet to ascend;
> The difficulty will not me offend.
> For I perceive the way to life lies here.
> Come, pluck up, heart; let's neither faint nor fear.
> Better, though difficult, the right way to go,
> Than wrong, though easy, where the end is woe.

The challenging climb of confession, although it begins with a descent, will be worth it. Abundant life, joyful forgiveness and intimate fellowship are found at the end of its journey, which, it turns out, is more of a walk.

The first (implicit) instruction in John's letter is to 'walk in the light' (1 John 1.7). In many ways, it's a synonym for confession (coming out from hiding in the dark). It is bookended by its matching opposite, the last verse of the letter, possibly the oldest surviving apostle's final words: 'Little children, keep yourselves from idols' (1 John 5.21). Together they speak to what the choice of confession is all about.

Idols are not just inanimate Buddha-like statues. Lloyd-Jones says they are 'anything in our lives that occupies the place that should be occupied by God alone . . . anything that holds my life and my devotion . . . anything to which I give much of my time and attention, my energy and my money; anything that holds a controlling position in my life is an idol'.[4]

In the Introduction we mentioned King David's adultery and murder; have you ever wondered what his idols might have been that caused him to stuff up so badly? We're no historical mind readers, but our best guess would be some combination of sex, power, control, comfort and reputation were at play. During the time when kings were meant to go out to war and serve on the battlefield,[5] David was indulging himself in the bedroom. Then he embarked on a campaign of lying and murder to protect his name. The Miss Tanorexic question needs to be put again here (see Introduction, page 3). Are we really so much more sophisticated 3,000 years later that we don't end up worshipping similar idols and succumbing to similar temptations (seen through the lens of the Sermon on the Mount)[6] of lust and anger, for example? We don't think so, if our own lives are anything to go by.

Idols are sneaky. It's not just that they don't look like cliché objects of worship. They also make seductive promises, which they don't actually have the power or good intentions to keep. Consider *The Matrix*, a film in which artificial intelligence has defeated humanity and machines use people like batteries. They keep humans under control by plugging them into a false, computer-generated reality called the Matrix. Everything humans see, smell and hear is part of this virtual construct that isn't real. A computer program stimulates their brains and deceives them into thinking they're living normal lives – eating, sleeping, working and interacting together – whilst in fact they are being harvested for their bioelectrical energy. A handful of people escape and are working to set others free, but one of them, Cypher, betrays his friends. He wants to live the rest of his life in the Matrix as a rich, important, famous person (the idols he thinks the machines can give him). In a face-to-face negotiation at a restaurant in the Matrix, Cypher says: 'I know this steak doesn't exist. I know that when I put it in my mouth, the Matrix is telling my brain that it is juicy and delicious. After nine years, you know what I realise? . . . Ignorance is bliss.' He chooses to live the lie (think: denial) rather than face reality (think: confession) but . . . here's the thing. The machines almost certainly had no intention of honouring the deal. Cypher chose wrong.

I know this personally. For years my idol was physical beauty. I obsessed about being better looking. If my nose, ears, hair were like this, or like that person's, then I would be successful and adored. I even endured painful cosmetic surgery, but on the day of the big reveal, I wasn't satisfied and started to plan my next operation.[7]

Idols, whether money, sex and power or fame, family and fortune, just string you along. It's like watching episode after episode of the TV show *Lost* as it drip-feeds you crumbs of curiosity that promise some great feast of meaning. But at the end, after 121 episodes, it's a damp squib of disappointment – and you realise you just wasted no small part of your life.[8]

Our worship of idols is sin because only God is worthy of our worship. And sin, as my old pastor[9] used to say, always takes you further than you want to go, keeps you longer than you want to stay and costs you more than you want to pay.

Confession is a choice, much like the wisdom literature of the book of Proverbs. You can choose to walk with sexy Lady Folly or saintly Lady Wisdom. Or to put it the *Bridget Jones' Diary* way, you can choose handsome, womanising boss Daniel Cleaver (Hugh

Grant) and be cheated on, or you can choose cute, kind, gets-better-as-you-get-to-know-him Mark Darcy (Colin Firth) and experience real devotion and faithfulness. Cue Prov. 28.13: 'Whoever conceals their sins does not prosper, but the one who confesses and renounces them finds mercy.'[10]

You can choose the way of flourishing or floundering, confessing or concealing. Which will it be? Our hope, of course, is that you'll say yes and daily confess, because your prosperity but also your community's prosperity depends on it. That's because if we want to minister powerfully to the place where we are, which for us is London, we must free ourselves from the idols of London (insert your village, town, city here) – 'so that you may become blameless and pure, children of God without fault in a warped and crooked generation. Then you will shine among them like stars in the sky' (Phil. 2.15 NIV).

Choices are important; as leadership guru John Maxwell put it: 'Life is a matter of choices and every choice makes you.'[11] So again, we ask, as we daily commit sin, which 'you' will you be? Real and flourishing through confessing? Or fake and floundering through denying?

Facing our true selves, owning the bad stuff we do (sins of commission) and the good stuff we fail to do (sins of omission, like the priest and the Levite in the parable of the Good Samaritan,[12] who walk on by the robbed, half-dead man on the side of the road), can be painful. That's why the word *if* isn't just a choice, it's also a divine promise of forgiveness, giving absolute assurance of confession's awesome outcome.

The promise

If you confess (we'll cover what the word *confess* means in chapter 3, but for now just think of it as agreeing with God about how ugly your sin is), God says, I guarantee you will be forgiven. If you do this, then this *will* happen. It's a divine cause-and-effect relationship that cannot be broken. Confession's reward isn't uncertain like losing weight daily on a diet, which can be more random than playing the lottery. Its prize is guaranteed.

How is that possible? Looking just two verses back, it's because of 'the blood of Jesus' (1 John 1.7). In the words of another apostle, Peter: 'Christ also suffered once for sins, the righteous for the unrighteous, that he might bring us to God, being put to death in the flesh but made alive in the spirit' (1 Peter 3.18). It's possible because of the historical death and resurrection of Jesus, to which John was an eyewitness. He very deliberately emphasises this in the opening verses of his first letter. 'We have seen . . . looked upon . . . touched with our hands . . . seen . . . seen . . . heard,' he says. This is no untestable *private* encounter (noting Islam and Mormonism's origins) but a public, verifiable revelation of God's love. Jesus's life, death and resurrected body were observed by hundreds, maybe thousands. This is even picked up on by sources outside of the Bible.[13]

This public, historical verifiability makes Christianity unique. It means that the promise of forgiveness is not wishful thinking, hoping for the best from a capricious wannabe deity who may or may not say yes. No, it is written by God in blood in a revolutionary historical act of love that he will never take back. Hear John's eyewitness testimony. Hear the testimony of men and women in the New Testament Scriptures who were willing to die for their belief in what they'd seen, and let it fill you with confidence.[14] Why would they 'waste' their lives bringing death to themselves and their families if it weren't true?

It's a thought that provoked a not-as-short-as-we-think Frenchman, Emperor Napoleon Bonaparte.[15] Toward the end of his life, after forty victories in battle and six million Europeans dead, exiled to the island of St Helena, he reflected on this willingness to die, alongside his own place in history: 'I know men, and I tell you, Jesus Christ is no mere man. Between him and every other person in the world, there is no possible term of comparison. Alexander, Caesar,

Charlemagne and I myself have founded great empires; but upon what did these creations of our genius depend? Upon force. Jesus alone founded His empire upon love, and to this very day millions would die for Him . . .'[16]

You can be confident – no, certain – that when you confess you will be forgiven because 2,000 years ago Jesus, who was himself God, became an atoning sacrifice for your sins. He took the guilt, shame, grime and stain of your sin so you can be forgiven and clean. Let's reflect again on *The Shawshank Redemption* to see this more clearly. We often think of ourselves as the main character, Andy Dufresne, and as we wrote in the Introduction, there's some truth in that, but we think we're also like his fellow inmate Red, and Andy is actually a bit like Jesus.

There was always something mysterious, God-like, about Andy. Red, played by Morgan Freeman, describes him as strolling like a man in a park, at peace, despite walking through and experiencing first-hand one of the most brutal prisons in America, 'like he had on an invisible coat that would shield him from this place'. There's also the supernatural way Andy perfectly puts back the Rita Hayworth poster – from inside his tunnel – to hide the hole in his prison cell wall as he begins his escape.

Red says, 'Andy crawled to freedom through 500 hundred yards of [expletive]-smelling foulness I can't even imagine . . . and maybe I just don't want to . . . 500 yards, that's the length of five football fields, just shy of half a mile . . .' Think about what that would have been like, then multiply it by infinity. Now you're beginning to understand what Jesus willingly went through when he was covered in the human excrement of the world, our sin, so that by faith in him, we can be clean.

Andy broke out, but not just to set himself free but to win freedom for his friend Red, who was close to losing hope. Will Red go the way of Brooks, who committed suicide after his release from prison a few years earlier, or will he say yes to Andy's invitation? Red sets off in hope and follows the clues Andy has left for him, resulting in a beautiful (rewritten) ending narrated by Red. These are the final words of the film: 'I find I'm so excited I can barely sit still or hold a thought in my head. I think it's the excitement only a free man can feel, a free man at the start of a long journey whose conclusion is uncertain. I hope I can make it across the border. I hope to see my friend and shake his hand. I hope the Pacific is as blue as it has been in my dreams. I hope.'[17]

If Andy is a bit like Jesus and Red is a bit like us, this is a bit like confession, but with confession the ending is certain. You *can* cross the border to the divine. You *can* walk with Jesus, and the ocean, the width, length, height and depth of God's love, *is* immeasurably better than you hoped it would be.

Andy doesn't break Red out of physical prison, he breaks him out of an internal, mental, spiritual prison. This is similar to how Jesus sets us free, not necessarily in the way we expect but in the way we need most – from sin, to walk in fellowship with him, free from the cruel control of idols, throwing off everything that hinders joy. Don't delay putting this understanding into practice. Cross the border now. Reflect on the questions below and slowly, word by word, meditate with fresh eyes on the prayer of confession in Ps. 139.23–4 and journey deeper into God's forgiving love.

Questions for reflection

What are the pros and cons of choosing confession?

How should the *promise* of forgiveness encourage you to make the daily *choice* of confession?

Prayer of Confession
Search me, O God, and know my heart!
Try me and know my thoughts!
And see if there be any grievous way in me,
and lead me in the way everlasting!
Ps. 139.23–4

Forgiveness story #2

BERYL

I'd been away from church for several years, despite having grown up in a Christian home. You see, I'd met someone – a fun-loving, handsome Irishman – and we were sleeping together, even though I knew, deep down, it was wrong.

I felt guilty and ashamed, but every day I worked hard to keep those feelings at bay. Everyone else is doing it, so why can't we? He makes me feel special. Am I not entitled to that? But there was something inside I couldn't shake. Longing. Absence. Darkness. Despite all my attempts to tell myself otherwise, I didn't feel clean.

I called my old church pastor and met him secretly after a service, with my boyfriend. He suggested we try going to church for six weeks. I didn't think anything would happen and assumed I'd be off doing my own thing again soon but . . . As the pastor preached on temptation at one of those evening services, I could feel myself squirming uncomfortably under a horrible weight of conviction. I was fighting with myself. I knew my heart wasn't right. I knew I needed to give in, give my boyfriend up and get right with God. I was scared to surrender but knew I just had to.

At the end of the message I stood up in response to an 'altar call', an invitation to own my sin, come to the front, leave that old life behind and find forgiveness. As I walked forward, I felt a huge burden lift off me. What followed was an extraordinary sense of relief. The weight of guilt, the dirty baggage I had been carrying around with me, had been taken from me by Jesus. What's more, as I was coming forward, quite independently, so was my boyfriend; he almost knocked me over rushing down the aisle to respond. That same conviction had gripped him! We're now very happily married!

Despite having felt so dirty, when we got married, I proudly wore a cream wedding dress because I knew that God had cleaned me up and sorted me out. I was forgiven and so happy I'd confessed my sin, and confession continues today to be a joyful way I connect with God and celebrate my 'white as snow' (Isa. 1.18) child of God identity.

2
We

'[Christianity] is one beggar telling another beggar where to get food.'

D.T. Niles, *That They May Have Life*

Arrogant. This is a common criticism levelled against Christianity. A writer in HuffPost put it like this: 'To suggest that 1 out of 4,200 religions holds all of the truth and the key to salvation is not only arrogant, it is spiritually narcissistic.'[1]

Now, we know Christians can be arrogant – sorry. Hey, we know we ourselves have been – sorry again[2] – but we must point out that in making his statement, the author, ironically, is guilty of the arrogance he attributes to Christians.

First, he assumes the set of beliefs he holds about the world by which he makes this claim are not religious in any way. This is a bit like claiming not to speak with an accent – to assume other people have one but you don't.

Second, he assumes all religions are the same, which is rather judgemental. It's like saying 'if you've been to one African country, you've been to them all'. Or 'all Chinese people look alike'. Are you cringing? We hope so. Why are those any different than when Christianity is categorised as just another religion, often by people who know very little about what different religions actually teach?

Two illustrations are typically given: blindfolded people (imagine adherents to different religions) feeling different parts of an elephant, thinking they're feeling the whole, and pilgrims taking different routes up the same transcendent mountain. These thought experiments seem clever but actually – you guessed it – they're arrogant. The teller assumes they themselves are not blindfolded and can see the whole, that they are the one at the top of the mountain looking down in judgement, putting themselves in the place of God.

It's understandable why people might want to iron out the differences between religions. We want to avoid disagreement that could lead to conflict, even violence. We believe all people have equal value, but that doesn't mean all ideas have equal merit or have to agree with each other. Not everything can be 'capital T' Truth (compared to 'little t' truth, which is more of a personal preference, like not liking Brussels sprouts). 'Capital T' Truth is stubborn; if it's true, then everything else in contradiction to it, by definition, must be false. You are either a human being or the first aardvark who can read. You cannot be both human and aardvark. If that didn't do it for you, then try this: when I stand on our bathroom scales, they say 73.5 kg. I'd like them to say 65 kg. I could pretend they say what I want them to, but that wouldn't be true. They read 73.5 kg, which means all other weights are wrong. Are our scales arrogant? We don't think so.

The illustration breaks down, however, because it's not as if some religions are just one or two kilograms apart. No, they're radically different. It's more like kilograms versus metres per second, measuring different things altogether, or measuring nothing at all. Some postulate the existence of one God, others hundreds of gods, some no God; they differ dramatically on what 'salvation' is or means, let alone what you have to do to obtain it. Knowing these differences is an important step in our understanding of confession, especially for those less familiar with competing religions, to help us better see and savour it in comparison to disappointing alternatives, as well as encouraging us to hold firm to what we believe. But before we touch on them, we need to get to the main reason why Christianity isn't arrogant: its radical inclusivity.

'We', not 'you'

John was one of Jesus' closest disciples. He was the last surviving apostle. He saw Jesus' ministry up close and personal. He laid his head on Jesus' chest at the Last Supper. He was entrusted by Christ at the crucifixion to care for Jesus' mother Mary. He ate fish with the resurrected Lord. He became a prominent leader in the early Church and suffered in exile on the island of Patmos. He was privileged to write a significant portion of the New Testament, a biography, three letters and Revelation. This John does not say 'if *you* [inferior underlings] confess'. No, he uses the first-person plural in the original Greek, 'if *we* confess'. This is no hierarchical 'some are better than others' belief system. This is, in the words of Sri Lankan bishop D.T. Niles, 'one beggar telling another beggar where to get food'.[3] Christianity is the humble 'we', not 'you', faith. We're all in the gutter together. In the words of the transformed Christian-killer, the great preacher Paul, 'all have sinned and fall short of the glory of God' (Rom. 3.23).

'We' means 'me'

It's surely at least a little arrogant to argue you're the exception to this universal declaration. That, however, is what some people who infiltrated the Christian community John was addressing did. The departure of this proud, snobbish group of people referred to in 1 John 2.19 got folks down. Their super-spiritual claims made the average believer feel rubbish, to the point they may have even questioned their own salvation. So John tackles their false teaching head-on to encourage the Church. Three times John reports what the leavers said in chapter 1. 'If we claim,' verse 6. 'If we claim,' verse 8. 'If we claim,' verse 10. The leavers claimed intimacy with God whilst committing infidelity against him. They claimed to have no sin, making the cross redundant. They weren't honest with themselves about their own transgressions, like the three 'wise' monkeys who see no evil, speak no evil and hear no evil, denying their sin one sense at a time.

Newsflash: you can't hide from the truth of your sinfulness, no matter how hard you try. Consider American Joe Chandler.[4] He refused to find out who won the 2016 Clinton–Trump presidential election. He didn't want to ruin his mood. He worked from home, avoiding television, newspapers and social media. He walked around with headphones on and a sign around his neck: 'I don't know who won, and don't want to. Please don't tell me.' Amazingly, he survived for two weeks before his bubble of ignorance burst. Likewise, your sin will catch up with you one way or another. One of the greatest preachers of the nineteenth century, Charles Spurgeon, is said to have brilliantly burst the bubble of a man who claimed to be without sin. Spurgeon decided the quickest and best way to bring the man back to his senses was to stamp hard on his toe. Quickly getting an abusive, *sinful* reaction, Spurgeon proved the point.[5]

The truth is: we all need our bubbles burst and toes stamped. Like an angry, deluded *X Factor* contestant, we all find it hard to accept how bad we are. So, from time to time, we think it helps to take the Ten Commandments quiz.[6] Do you love things with more passion and commitment than you love God? It's OK, you don't have to answer out loud (we're not listening). We know it's almost certainly yes anyway. Do you live without due reverence for God? That's true of everyone. Have you ever told a lie? Be careful how you answer that. Now, you may not have committed adultery, but if we were gambling people, we'd bet a million pounds you've lusted over a sexy image of another person or looked twice at an attractive passer-by, right? We wonder if we paid someone to hack your browser history – or your brain, if that were possible – what we'd find. You're not a murderer either, we suspect, but you've been angry enough that for a split second, if a suitable weapon had been on hand, you just might have killed your horrible boss, that noisy neighbour, incompetent driver, inconsiderate tourist blocking your way or – dare we write it? – an irritating church member. Guilty? Us too! To think otherwise would be pride – a major sin, itself needing confession. According to C.S. Lewis in *Mere Christianity*, 'the essential vice, the utmost evil, is Pride. Unchastity, anger, greed, drunkenness, and all that, are mere flea bites in comparison: it was through Pride that the devil became the devil: Pride leads to every other vice: it is the complete anti-God state of mind'.[7] We are all guilty of it. 'We' means 'me'. We're all in the gutter and need a way out.

Where else can *we* go?

We all have a guilt problem that needs an answer. To what or whom can we go? When you survey the options out there, it's clear there's nowhere and no one else to turn to but Jesus.[8] Seeing the answer of Christian confession against the backdrop of dissatisfying solutions should awaken greater appreciation for the way out God has provided, giving more motivational momentum for us to get confessing.

Humanism, according to the American Humanist Association, rejects the very notions of sin and guilt.[9] Teachers of **Buddhism** say it doesn't do guilt.[10] Guilt is a dysfunctional aspect of our minds, in their opinion. Together with **Hinduism**, they typically advocate the 'what goes around comes around' doctrine of karma. 'Sin' becomes a breach of an impersonal principle rather than an offence against the personal Creator God, a breach that can only be dealt with by enduring the necessary amount of suffering the 'sin' deserves in this life – and in the life to come, if you don't suffer enough this time around, for what you (if you can call yourself 'you', because you don't really have any memory of this previous version of you) did in a past life.[11] But think of a child born blind, suffering, we understand, for 'sins' he or she cannot know about in this life (and therefore never be sure of not committing again), and without knowing how long the cycle has been going. Worse, any attempt to alleviate the suffering would only postpone the full suffering needed to satisfy the demands of karma. Karma sounds, well, pretty cruel, from our point of view.

What about **Islam**? Sure, it offers forgiveness, through obeying its conditions of *tawbah* (repentance) – but you cannot be certain of forgiveness. It hangs in the balance. This uncertainty is consistent with Islam's doctrine of salvation, by the way: that your good will hopefully outweigh the bad on the scales of divine justice.[12] That's not dissimilar to several branches of **Judaism**. It's a strategy we all adopt, actually, proudly trying to cover our guilt with good deeds. But isn't all the good we do polluted by impure motives and immoral behaviour? There is no truly altruistic human act.

When I (Holly) was growing up, I took to heart the saying 'an apple a day keeps the doctor away'. I carefully counterbalanced the number of Easter eggs I ate with Golden Delicious apples. But sadly, our bodies don't work that way, and all I got was a stomach ache and an unhappy dentist. The same is true for the health of our souls – we can add as many acts as we like, but none of them remove the sin that's already there. We all agreed that a drunk driver killing your child was wrong; would they still be in the wrong if last week they had donated their kidney to a family member? Of course! The kidney generosity is great, but it doesn't remove or replace the selfish drunken choice they made in driving.

Finally, **escapism**. Okay, so this isn't an established religion, but it's a remedy pursued religiously by many – self-medicating with anything from comfort eating or alcohol binging to fantasising about a different life to self-harm. These are damaging forms of distraction. In fact, we could argue that they're an unconscious and sometimes even conscious form of self-punishment, to atone for guilt. But how could you ever be sure if your efforts had been effective?

The way out of the gutter of guilt is not trying to climb out of it ourselves; we'll just slip over our sin on the way and fall on our proud faces. True forgiveness can be found in the One who doesn't just say he's forgiving but literally embodies it. He gets into the gutter with us to drink up its guilt, every drop of our disobedience, down to the last dregs. Jesus, God, consumed this cup of wrath[13] – the punishment for sin we deserve – by letting himself be tortured in our place on the gruesome cross. Lord, where else can we go?

Experience the same intimacy the great apostle John had with Jesus through confession by stopping and praying right now. If you're not sure what to say, use Clement of Rome's first-century prayer below to guide you. In modern Western culture, novelty and youth rule the day, and our constant search for authenticity can wrongly drive us only towards newness rather than looking back and benefitting from the hard work of those who've gone before us. This and the other historical confessions in this book are our privileged opportunity to learn from our great-great-and-many-more-great-grandparents in the faith.

If we want to love others well, the instruction John gives at least twelve times in his letter, we need to see how great God's excruciating act of extraordinary love is. God will not turn away anyone who will humbly approach him. Seeing the sin (log) in our own eyes and confessing it will help us be less nasty about the sin (speck) in another's, loving them out of the first love we have received from the God who is love. But what does 'confessing it' look like? That takes us to chapter 3.

Questions for reflection

In what way(s) does the practice of confession answer the accusation that Christianity is arrogant?

How can seeing that Jesus has the best answer to the problem of guilt help you to savour (and therefore practise) confession more?

Prayer of Confession

Thou didst make to appear the enduring fabric of the world by the works of Thy hand; Thou, Lord, didst create the earth on which we dwell – Thou, who art faithful in all generations, just in judgements, wonderful in strength and majesty, with wisdom creating and with understanding fixing the things which were made, who art good among them that are being saved and faithful among them whose trust is in Thee; O merciful and compassionate One, forgive us our iniquities and offences and transgressions and trespasses. Reckon not every sin of Thy servants and handmaids, but Thou wilt purify us with the purification of Thy truth, and direct our steps that we may walk in holiness of heart and do what is good and well-pleasing in Thy sight and in the sight of our rulers. Yea, Lord, make Thy face to shine upon us for good in peace, that we may be shielded by Thy mighty hand and delivered from every sin by Thine uplifted arm, and deliver us from those who hate us wrongfully. Give concord and peace to us and all who dwell upon the earth, even as Thou gavest to our fathers, when they called upon Thee in faith and truth, submissive as we are to Thine almighty and all-excellent name. Amen.

Clement of Rome, end of the first century

Forgiveness story #3

SHIN

My journey to freedom has been a long one. A constant battle between my flesh and my spirit to choose God, to receive his grace and to accept that I cannot win the struggle in my own strength. But throughout the complex web of drifting between intimacy and estrangement with God, he has shown me how unwavering and faithful his love and commitment to me are. Every time I have run back to him through honest confession, he has welcomed me in without shame and called me to stay.

I grew up in a Catholic family in the Philippines, knowing God was there but not having a relationship with Jesus. As a college student, I entered a singing competition on TV. To my delight, I won. No one had prepared me for what came next. My whole life changed overnight. I was now someone every person in the street recognised, but someone my family didn't. I was a really mean girl. I suddenly had so many opportunities, this money and power – it went to my head and I couldn't handle it.

Eventually, through a man I was dating, I found myself at a Christian church weeping as the sermon spoke straight to my selfish but bruised heart. Shortly afterwards I prayed with him to give God my life, but it felt so unreal. He told me all I had to do was invite God in, but it felt like it required more. That night I had a dream – I was surrounded by my bodyguards, but this time they didn't make me feel safe, they were trying to get me. As I was running away from them, I saw a small window, and I knew it was the only way out. I barged through and was met by a party celebrating – 'You are finally here!' I was safe. There was a woman at the party I couldn't get out of my head. Some weeks later when I attended my first Bible study, there she was! A stranger from my dream sat in front of me. I wept. God had proven his power. He was at work even when I didn't feel like it. I could trust him more than my feelings.

It wasn't a smooth journey for me. Whilst I connected with a church, God showed me I couldn't work my way back to him because I backslid again. I got so busy I let God drop out of my life. But just as before, that vacuum in my heart returned, and I called the church mentor I'd been ignoring and asked if we could start afresh. She cried and said she had been praying for me to ask that for a long time. Not long after, I was baptised.

You'd have thought that would have sealed the deal, but when I took a job in a London show to escape the pressure to perform in the Philippines, I ended up somehow leaving God behind too. I stopped praying and reading my Bible; my attendance at church was sporadic. I was a believer, but we were definitely 'on a break' at my end. I felt empty. I went through a string of bad relationships as I tried to clutch at people who would fill the hole. One day I felt so awful I committed to a fresh start. I cut off all distractions, even relationships, and went back to the Philippines and then on to a job in a show in New York.

I met a group of people at a church there who walked and prayed with me. I did a course at this church that helped me deal with the things that were holding me back from truly following God. At the course's retreat day, I finally let go of trying to make myself better. Instead, I confessed my sins and I opened my heart to God again and finally let him in to the baggage I had carried for so long. I felt so free. I experienced such joy.

I used to hide when I knew I was in the wrong, from others and from God. Now I don't. I know I don't need to withdraw because, when I am open and honest with God about my failings, he gladly forgives me, so I don't live under shame anymore. My nickname Shin means 'new heart' and that is what confession and God's forgiveness give me.

3

Confess

'In confession there occurs a breakthrough to the cross.'
Dietrich Bonhoeffer, *Life Together*

Have you ever forgotten to take the bin out? When we forget, or rather when I forget,[1] we know about it. Our kitchen stinks! You can't smell anything apart from dirty nappies (literally – at the time of writing one of our kids is still wearing them). No spices, flowers or freshly baked bread can overpower the biohazard stench. Failing to confess is like not taking the bin out – the stench of guilt blocks out the aroma of Christ; you lose fellowship with God. This is the context of 1 John 1.9: fellowship, fellowship, fellowship, fellowship. We've written it four times because John wrote it four times in the verses leading up to 1 John 1.9. Fellowship, not salvation, is repeated, and fellowship is about close companionship with the God of joy (noticing, as we said already, that the perfection of joy is the first purpose statement of John's letter).

In the words of the brilliant pastor–theologian Dietrich Bonhoeffer: 'In confession there occurs a breakthrough to the cross.'[2] Confession is the key that unlocks the treasure chest a person receives when they cross the line of faith. Too many Christians live as spiritual paupers when God has given them the code of confession to enter and rejoice inside the enormous vault of God's abundant love and mercy.

So *what* exactly is confession? We're glad you asked. One of our favourite confession definitions comes from seventeenth-century English Puritan Thomas Manton. 'Confession,' he said, 'is an act of mortification; it is as it were the vomit of the soul.'[3] To confess is to be sick, to puke out the evil toxins of sin that are poisoning your soul.

But this isn't a private exercise between you and your impersonal toilet, of course; confession is relational. So before we get more into the *what* – what confession is – let's firstly consider the *who*. Whom are we meant to confess to?

Who?

Plants? That's what some very misguided theology students did in New York, September 2019. Union Seminary tweeted: 'Today in chapel, we confessed to plants. Together, we held our grief, joy, regret, hope, guilt and sorrow in prayer; offering them to the beings who sustain us but whose gift we too often fail to honor. What do you confess to the plants in your life?'[4] That's silly; they're not even sentient. The plants, we mean. Sorry, that was unkind. We understand the need to confess our poor stewardship of the planet entrusted to us, only not to plants, a creation, but to their Creator.

Should you confess to a priest, then? No, because through faith in Christ, the Son, we have been given direct access to God, the Father. That's arguably what the book of the Bible called Hebrews is primarily about: our privileged *access*. We can personally approach God's throne of grace with boldness.[5]

What about to another person? Yes, we are instructed by James (Jesus' initially sceptical half-brother who became a leader in the Church after Christ's resurrection) to 'confess [our] sins to each other' (Jas. 5.16). But the context there (as the 'Therefore' suggests) is probably more about reconciliation between people. James moves from healing in an individual's body to healing in the body of Christ. It's an encouragement to confess and forgive each other for harm done to one another, e.g., to expel the bad spiritual infection of bitterness from churches. This is an important practice, as is the related discipline of being accountable to trusted persons about our sin, but it's not what John is writing about in his letter. Lloyd-Jones said, 'Surely it is unnecessary that I should emphasise here that not for one second at this point does John mention confessing my sins to anybody else; he is concerned about my fellowship with God, my walking with God.'[6] 1 John 1.9 is primarily about confessing our sins to God.

What?

The Greek word for confess, *homolegeo*, means to say the same thing. In this context, it's to say the same thing as God about your sin, to agree it's viler than vomit. Sometimes it's helpful to understand what something is by seeing what it's not. The opposite of 'confess' in 1 John is 'deny' – we see that in 1 John 2.22–3, where the two words are used as contrasting opposites.

There's the bare-faced denial, let's call it the Shaggy defence – 'It wasn't me.'[7] President Clinton is a good example. 'I did not have sexual relations with that woman, Ms Lewinsky,' he famously said. When the evidence against him was overwhelming, he changed tack – 'Err, maybe I did,' as we paraphrase it – an admission but not a confession. Such denials are a variation of Adam's garden of Eden blame-shifting: the 'It was the woman *you* gave me' defence, accusing not just his wife but also God for creating her, in a deviously cunning double play. The truth is we're all chips off the old block; like Adam, we're masters at not accepting responsibility for our wrongdoing. In an article in *ShortList* titled 'How to Apologise Without Actually Apologising', writer Dave Fawbert says the non-apology apology has become popular because many of us deep down don't believe we've done anything wrong. He lists some examples.[8] Maybe you, like us, have said them.

- 'I'm sorry to anyone who was offended.' Meaning: I'm sorry you took offence but that doesn't mean it was offensive, just that you must be easily offended, so it's your fault.
- 'I'm sorry you feel that way.' Meaning: I'm sorry you're upset but other people weren't, so actually you must have the problem.

- 'Mistakes were made.' Meaning: by others but not by me.
- 'I'm only human.' Meaning: because we all make mistakes, none of us are responsible for them. Err, try saying that to a judge or jury in a criminal trial (there is such a thing as criminal negligence, by the way).

This is one way we typically approach God in confession; it's interesting to note that even our confessing can be tainted with sin. True confession, by contrast, begins with accepting responsibility. It is coming out from hiding, dragging your sins into the open and siding with God against them. It is not simply mourning the personal detrimental consequences of your sin, even with tears; that's worldly sorrow.[9] Think of Esau – he cried about his foolish profanity of selling his birthright, but his weren't tears of confession, only the pain of personal loss.[10] Or consider when Samuel calls Saul to account for his disobedience.[11] Saul eventually says, 'I have sinned' (1 Sam. 15.24), but he's not really bothered about his wrongdoing. All he seems to care about is his reputation, persuading Samuel to help him save face before the elders and people of Israel (noting also that he has recently set up a monument in his own honour).[12] Real confession is godly grief. It's rending your heart, not just your garments.[13] It's being cut to your core about the offence you caused God and the dishonour you've done him.[14] It's seeing the sinfulness of your sins through God's eyes and turning from them.

In this sense, confession and repentance are two sides of the same coin, at least in the context of 1 John 1.9. Prov. 28.13 concurs: 'Whoever conceals their sins does not prosper, but the one who *confesses and renounces* them finds mercy.'[15] 'Confesses and renounces' is quite possibly a hendiadys, one idea expressed through two words. Confession is not just about words but about turning away, forsaking action. You turn from walking in darkness to walk in the light.[16] This is what we see happening in the early Church, as recorded in Acts 19.18 (NIV). In a city called Ephesus in southern Turkey, 'many of those who believed now came and openly *confessed* their evil deeds'. Their confession is immediately followed by verse 19, which presents as part and parcel of their same event: 'A number who had practised sorcery brought their scrolls together and burned them *publicly*. When they calculated the value of the scrolls it came to 50,000 drachmas.' If our sums are correct, that would be £4.1 million today![17]

The impact of this, verse 20 says, was 'the word of the Lord spread widely and grew in power.' Their confession was evidence of radically transformed lives that trusted Jesus, not sorcery or money, and it became the talk of the whole region. The witness of holiness reveals the all-surpassing sufficiency of Jesus. Your vigilance against sin reveals Jesus' victory over it. It says to the world: 'Jesus is so much better than all the short-lived pleasures of sin.' Confessing means you stop caring about saving face and start savouring and showcasing grace.

That's the *what* of confession; how about the *when*?

When?

Confession should happen ASAP. We need to mind the gap; the time gap between the moment of sinning and confessing is a sign of how well you're walking with God, how tuned in you are. The shorter the gap, the better.

Confession should be a regular activity throughout every Christian's day because the more you walk in the light, with God who is light, the more of your sin you should see (and the more of his grace you can savour). This can be scary, even to the point where you may wonder whether you're really saved, a thought we believe some of those John was writing to had. Instead of your sin taking you to your knees in confession, you can let it crush you with condemnation. Don't let it do that – let's remember, 1 John isn't about questioning genuine salvation, it's about those who already believe[18] confidently experiencing the joy of restored and closer fellowship with God.[19]

Confession requires us to grow in sensitivity to the Holy Spirit's correction, convicting us of our sins.[20] If we can't think of anything to confess after we've invited God to search our hearts,[21] it could be that pride is stopping us from seeing our sins. Many of us are not aware when we have grieved the Holy Spirit. We're much like Mary and Joseph returning from Jerusalem to Nazareth, not realising Jesus, God, wasn't with them.[22] We don't readily notice when God's empowering presence has withdrawn, when we've fallen out of *fellowship* with him.

It is possible to disappoint God.[23] We wouldn't be commanded by Paul *not* to grieve the person[24] of the Holy Spirit in Eph. 4.30 if that weren't so. Again, this doesn't mean that if you lose this felt sense of God's presence (however you experience his nearness) you've lost your salvation. Neither does it mean the Holy Spirit can ever stop residing in you, because the verse continues by affirming that by faith you've been 'sealed [with the Spirit] for the day of redemption [when Christ comes again]'. The Holy Spirit will not abandon a child of God. What it does mean is bitterness, rage, anger, quarrels, slander, all forms of malice, unkindness and indifference (the surrounding context of the verse) can cause the *felt presence* of the Holy Spirit (for want of a better phrase), pictured as a dove coming upon Jesus at his baptism,[25] to become distant and even to figuratively fly away. The dove of the Holy Spirit brings assurance – supernatural power, peace, joy, a deep sense of how real God is and how loved his children are, making it hard to doubt.

Dr R.T. Kendall once said that the greatest teaching he came across in his twenty-five years of ministry at Westminster Chapel was that 'the easiest thing in the world is to grieve the Holy Spirit'. The dove is a very sensitive bird, he wisely pointed out, meaning the Holy Spirit is a very sensitive person (in a holy way, not a vulnerable human way). Sin distances us from his assuring presence; confession draws us back to his loving embrace.

When you confess your sins, you're inviting the Holy Spirit to come close. You taste that sweet assurance again of being a child of

God[26] and open the door to supernatural power to witness.[27] You are restoring *fellowship* with God. All the delightful expressions of God's love, all the experiences of his rejoicing in you, will no longer be withdrawn as he comes, embraces and tenderly enfolds you in the arms of his love once more.[28]

Too many, however, take a long time to confess and come to their senses – years can be wasted. For others, it can be months, weeks or days. Some have managed to cut it down to hours, minutes, even seconds. That's what we should all be working towards. To develop the illustration, it's sensing the wings of the dove flapping and getting ready to fly away. Then we can stop mid-sentence, confess, give a heartfelt apology for offending God and speak again, but this time with grace, inviting the Spirit 'down'.

I once sat in a pastoral session, I'm ashamed to say, feeling unrighteous anger with the person in front of me, who'd sinned spectacularly. Why had he been so foolish? Why wasn't he listening? Why was he taking up so much of my precious time? Didn't he know there were more important things I could be doing? Every bit of advice I gave fell to the ground. Every attempt to make progress was thwarted. Are you surprised? You shouldn't be: my irritable anger distanced me from the Holy Spirit, until the person in front of me said something that pulled at my heartstrings and helped me enter his pain. Suddenly I felt terrible. 'How arrogant I am,' I thought, 'for there but for the grace of God go I.' In a moment of quick confession, brought about by the grace of God, I was able to change my attitude and approach. I fellowshipped with the Holy Spirit (rather than my flesh) and the man in front of me had, I believe, a breakthrough moment with God, as the Holy Spirit came upon him.

It is very easy to grieve the Spirit. It happens to all of us all the time. We get angry and hold grudges about so many things, especially when we feel slighted. It can be anything, from being cut up in traffic to losing it with your kids to your boss not giving you the praise you think you deserve. Bitterness and anger send the dove figuratively flying. The question is, do you notice his wings flapping? Are you mindful of his presence? Do you sense his grief? This kind of deliberate noticing helps to narrow the gap.

Imagine what could happen if every follower of Jesus kept in fellowship with the Spirit. Revival!

How?

How can we stop being so deaf, dumb and blind to our sins and start noticing them more? One part of the answer is in the next chapter, 'Our Sins', which is about understanding what sin is and identifying the sins you're particularly guilty of committing. But something important must come first: seeing God, walking in the light of his glory. We need to see that 'God is light, and in him is no darkness at all' (1 John 1.5). Getting our eyes off ourselves and seeing God's perfection empowers confession because we begin to see just how far short of his glory we've fallen, but in the context of loving communion with him. This is what happened to Job, Isaiah and Peter, and it was good.

Job

Job suffered terribly. He lost his family and his fortune and was in physical agony. His 'friends' only added insult to injury by telling him he was being punished for sin. But we are told Job was 'blameless and upright' (Job 1.8), 'did not sin or charge God with wrong' (Job 1.22) and 'did not sin in what he said' (Job 2.8 NIV) to his wife. Job, however, did curse the day of his birth, his counsellors, his sores and even the ash heap he was sitting on.

In chapter 13, he impatiently demands that God explain the reason for his suffering. In chapters 38–41, God responds with question after question, about seventy-seven in total, demanding that Job answer *him*. Questions like: 'Where were you when I laid the foundation of the earth?' (Job 38.4). 'Have you commanded the morning since your days began, and caused the dawn to know its place?'

(Job 38.12). 'Can you bind the chains of the Pleiades?' (Job 38.31). Job is given a class in the creative beauty and brilliance of God. Seeing God in this way humbles him and helps him to confess his sin – proud presumption – and find peace again. Job responds, 'You said, "Listen now, and I will speak; I will question you, and you shall answer me." My ears had heard of you but now my eyes have seen you. *Therefore* I despise myself and repent in dust and ashes' (Job 42.4–6 NIV).[29] Job's confession results in restoration – 'the Lord blessed the latter days of Job more than his beginning' (Job 42.12).

Isaiah

Isaiah 'saw the Lord' (Isa. 6.1) when there was trouble abroad and disaster at home. The Assyrian war machine, fresh from victory in Arpad in Syria, was on its way. The military genius King Uzziah was dead. The nation was in moral disarray, calling evil 'good' and good 'evil'. At such a challenging time Isaiah saw the world's true king, God seated on the throne, ruling in majesty. Only it utterly floored him. He began bemoaning the sins of his nation; seeing God got him bemoaning his own. Our fireball sun is but a flickering candle flame in comparison to the burning, bright beauty of God's holy, holy, holiness (all-powerful, overwhelmingly unique beauty and goodness). That's why even the angels dare not look at him. They cover their faces.[30] Isaiah responds by pronouncing a curse upon himself: 'Woe is me!' (Isa. 6.5). Seeing the beauty of God's holiness leads Isaiah to see the ugliness of his sinfulness. The particular sin God's glory has shone its spotlight on is Isaiah's speech. 'I am a man of unclean lips,' he says (Isa. 6.5).

'Out of the abundance of the heart,' Jesus says in Matt. 12.34, 'the mouth speaks.' In verse 36, he says we'll have to give an account for every careless word we've ever spoken. So what does your mouth say about you? How will you explain the lies you've told or the gossip you've spread? There's 'a world of evil' in that there tongue of yours. That's what James wrote in chapter 3 of his letter. It only takes the spark of a carelessly or wrongly placed word to start a forest fire.

I discovered this many years ago, a year after finishing secondary school (that's high school, for any American readers). I received a death threat letter in the post, describing all the brutal things that would be done to me leading up to my death. My mum gave it to the police and they investigated. Several months later I found out it had been sent by a former classmate. The only thing I could think of that might have triggered it was a horrible comment I'd made about his appearance three years earlier. He'd forgotten his PE kit and had to go topless, or 'skins' as we called it. It was probably nothing more than a sentence I said that publicly humiliated him, but its poison must have festered for a long time, in what I hadn't known was an unhappy home environment. How I now wish I could take those words back and speak encouragement to him instead. Are you thinking before you speak? Using your words to bless or curse? To build up or tear down? To wound or heal?

But into the hopeless despair of Isaiah's guilt, God sends an angel with a burning coal from the temple altar – a picture of Jesus – sprinkled with blood from the sacrifices made above it, to take away his sin. Isaiah had done nothing to earn this; he deserved death, but instead, he received the kiss of life. Such unmerited favour led him to say in the face of his challenging call, 'Here am I. Send me' (Isa. 6.8).

Peter

'Put out into the deep' (Luke 5.4), Jesus said to Simon Peter, and let's catch some fish. 'It won't work,' we imagine the experienced fisherman to have said ('they're not biting, now is not a good time, we've been at it all night and the conditions aren't right,' he probably thought), 'but because you asked, we'll do it.' They caught such a large number of fish, not only did their nets break but two fishing boats became so full they began to sink! 'When Simon Peter saw this, he fell at Jesus' knees and looking up at Jesus said, "Depart from me, for I am a sinful man, O Lord"' (Luke 5.8). Peter saw the Creator-of-all-things' control over everything, and it led him to his knees in confession. He also experienced God's extraordinary compassion. It's likely that Peter was a man desperately trying to make ends meet (he'd been fishing all night!), struggling to get by in a society impoverished by oppressive Roman taxation. We see him full of doubts, angry at God for allowing his people to suffer. Fish = money. In this breathtaking moment, God gave him a catch that could pay off all his debts, give him some breathing room, some security for his family. Peter was so undone by such undeserved favour, he felt he couldn't be in Jesus' presence. 'How can he be so good to me,' he must have thought, 'a sinner?' But Jesus did the opposite of what Peter said – he invited Peter to follow him.

The greatness of God, however, is not only seen in looking up at his holy otherness but also in looking down at his humble service. Peter had another significant encounter that provoked confession. It was recorded by John, in chapter 13 of his first-century biography. With the unimaginable pressures of the cross just hours away, Jesus stoops to slave-like service. He washes his proud, argumentative disciples' feet, even Judas', the one who would betray him. This extraordinary act of humility by deity foreshadows the cross. When Peter finally gets this, he effectively says, in the spirit of confession, 'Wash not just my feet but all of me because every part of me is dirty with sin.'

Jesus explains his actions in verse 10: 'A person who has had a bath [that is, submersed themselves in me by believing in me] needs *only* to wash his feet [daily confess sins]; his whole body is clean [from the moment he believes].'[31] Take a moment or two to read that again.

Confession helps you to see, savour and celebrate God, not just by looking up to his infinite highness but by looking down, recoiling even, in amazement at the astonishing inappropriateness of his humiliating service. Peter's initial response, resisting Jesus washing his feet, wasn't all bad. In some ways, we pity followers of other so-called gods who can only look up at their alleged greatness. The glory of God is also seen, perhaps more greatly seen, in looking down, at the God who places himself at your feet. It's seeing the God of infinite highness embracing unimaginable lowness. Why? So he can wash not only your mind, body and soul once and for all but also your feet. It's a daily cleansing from the fellowship-disrupting filth of your 'foot' sins, walking where you shouldn't, trampling upon people to get what you want, standing still – not doing much to alleviate the suffering of others.

Seeing God's perfection empowers confession. It will help you to see your sin – our darkness is revealed in the light of his glory. But it will also help you to see the way out of sin – that his light can overcome that darkness. So to liberate the discipline of confession, you must fix your eyes on the author and perfecter of your faith. This means meditating on the Scriptures daily. Start with the encounters Job, Isaiah and Peter had. What do they tell you about God, and therefore yourself? Practise filling your mind with noble, right, pure, lovely, admirable, excellent and praiseworthy thoughts about God by seeing how he epitomises all of those and more[32] on every page of the Bible. This leads to true confession – being able to identify your sin, look the ugliness of it right in the face and then sock it right in the jaw with the indestructible wooden timbers of the cross.

Questions for reflection

What's the difference between true and false confession?

How can you shorten the gap between commission of sin and confession of sin?

How does seeing God's perfection empower confession?

What could you do to see God more clearly?

Prayer of Confession
Jesus, my feet are dirty. Come even as a slave to me, pour water into your bowl, come and wash my feet. In asking such a thing I know I am overbold, but I dread what was threatened when you said to me, 'If I do not wash your feet I have no fellowship with you.' Wash my feet then, because I long for your companionship.
Origen of Alexandria, c. 185–254

Forgiveness story #4

BEN

Pornography was my poison. I grew up in a pretty normal home. But a combination of the wrong friends, cannabis, underachievement and, most of all, porn meant that I was far from flourishing. I wasn't a believer. I'd met Christians, I even wanted to become one, but I thought there was no way I could. I just had too many bad things in my life.

To my surprise, however, God met with me. I heard him speaking – not audibly, but a voice inside me, in a way I hadn't known before. He said, 'I have conquered all of that.' He meant my sin. It made me weep tears of sorrow and laugh for joy all at the same time. It was an emotionally sweet experience – a wonderful sense of lightness, having felt so crushed before. I was forgiven, but the shadow of pornography remained for another fourteen years. Why? I don't know. Some people seem to have a complete breakthrough when they cross the line of faith, but that wasn't to be my story.

The compulsion to look kept coming. I would give in to it even though I knew it would end up making me feel worse. When the pressures of life got the better of me, I would concede and drink its battery-acid poison for that short time of feeling accepted, loved and powerful, even though it was, of course, all false. The images were photoshopped. The women had to be paid to look happy. Some could even have been trafficked. It's horrible to think about it.

I could see the damage it was doing, in my friendships with other believers, whom I could never open up to for fear that they might find out, and, of course, in the early years of my marriage. I made the woman I'd promised to love feel like she wasn't good enough every time she found out. So I tried to cover it up when I could. I'd pretend I wasn't feeling well, for example, so we couldn't go on our date night that evening. The truth was, I just felt horribly ashamed and unworthy of her love because I'd binged on porn again. I could also see the damage it was doing to my relationship with God. I spent most of my time, like Adam and Eve, hiding from him after eating the forbidden fruit.

The moment of breakthrough came not so much from confessing my sins of pornography, although that did help, but from confessing the sins beneath them. The deep transformation came from believing that what God said in Scripture was true. That he had forgiven me. That his grace was sufficient for me. That I didn't have to perform to impress him, and so I didn't need to medicate myself with porn to alleviate the deep sense of failure and inadequacy I had about myself. I reached the point where I was finally able to authentically confess my proud unbelief. You see, I didn't really believe that what God said about me in the Bible – that he loves me despite my sin – was true. I rated my view of myself as more trustworthy than my Creator's. Getting down to this deep taproot of sin, arrogantly putting myself in the place of God, brought real freedom and joy. Sharing this confession with a trusted friend cemented it powerfully. I wasn't hiding from God or man now.

Seeing God's love and faithfulness, knowing he won't reject me but forgive me when I genuinely confess, has so encouraged me. I own my sin sooner and get back up quicker when I have given in to these destructive ways again, rather than wallow in self-pity. Each time I fall now, I come back stronger, my burden gets lighter, the temptation seems weaker and my gratitude for God is greater. Regular confession is helping me overcome and win the battle against sin.

4

Our sins

'Sin is:
The glory of God not honored.
The holiness of God not reverenced.
The greatness of God not admired . . .'

John Piper

Know your enemy. That, according to military strategist Sun Tzu, is one of the most basic rules of warfare. There have been many times when I have seriously underestimated my opponents. Growing up, I was an arrogant teenage tennis player. I thought I could beat every girl at tennis, until I was thrashed by one and embarrassingly passed out through physical exhaustion trying to hold my own against another. Pride literally came before a fall in that instance. Thanks to these experiences, I am not foolish enough, like 12% of men in the UK, to think I could win a point in a game of tennis against twenty-three-time Grand Slam winner Serena Williams.[1] To expose such stupidity, Serena agreed to take on not just one average man but six on the opposing side of the net. She destroyed them.[2]

When it comes to spirituality, many of us don't just underestimate our enemy; we don't even know we're at war. Professor Richard Lovelace said: 'Much of the church's warfare today is fought by blindfolded soldiers who cannot see the forces ranged against them.'[3] Consider how people responded to the coronavirus pandemic, which has taken hundreds of thousands of lives, caused global economic hardship and led to social distancing measures that seemed to be in place forever. We think there were a lot of people, at least in the UK, who were initially blasé about it, assuming we wouldn't get it as bad as other countries. Many carried on their lives as normal until the scary realisation came that COVID-19 was already here, marching against us, with exponential life-taking effect. We all had to rapidly move to a wartime mindset to combat this invisible enemy.

We believe a similar shift is required in the Church today towards the greatest invisible enemies. This is the ultimate kind of 'wokeness' our world needs. We must better understand whom and what we're up against. Drum roll, or rather chilling sound effect, please: the war you are fighting, whether you realise it or not, is against the unholy alliance of the world, the flesh and the devil, and the way they work together to ensnare, entangle and exterminate you (and everyone you know) with sin.

The world

The world is always seeking to squeeze you into its sinful ways of thinking.[4] We need only two words to make our case: skinny jeans. I initially thought they were effeminate and extremely uncomfortable looking. I said I would never wear them. But today I'm not only wearing them, I like them. I even dare to think they just about make me look cool. The fashion world has squeezed me into its mould. Where else have I – we – gone with the flow of majority thinking on far more important matters, like morality? When it comes to sin, are we in danger of calling evil 'good' and good 'evil' because that's what popular media and secular university professors are saying?[5]

The world is like an elite 'black hat' hacker that is constantly seeking to break into your mental mainframe with its malignant code. This is not too different from one of those annoying earworms, songs that get into your head so you can't stop singing them, using up more RAM on them than you'd like to admit. Rick Astley's song 'Never Gonna Give You Up' is a good example.[6] Sorry if you've got it stuck in your head now.

The flesh

The flesh is always tempting you to succumb to its sinful cravings. When a person, through faith in Jesus, is made spiritually alive, it's not just their mental software that gets upgraded. They're given a whole new God-empowered operating system to run the hardware of their yet to be fully redeemed body, also known as the flesh. Yes, the flesh, as the Apostle Paul wrote in Rom. 6.6, has been 'crucified with [Christ], in order that the body of sin might be brought to nothing'. But in the words of the great reformer John Calvin, 'there remains in regenerate man a smouldering cinder of evil from which desires continually leap forth to allure and spur him to commit sin'.[7] These enslaving desires can be anything from sugar to pornography, from praise to power. They keep company with treacherous impulses within us, like judgementalism and indifference to injustice. That's why Paul goes on to say, 'Let not sin therefore reign in your mortal body, to make you obey its passions. Do not present your members to sin as instruments for unrighteousness, but present yourselves to God as those who have been brought from death to life' (Rom. 6.12–13a).

It is a frightening truth that 'your enemy is not only upon you but in you also'; that there is a 'living coal continually'[8] in the body that is your house that if not attended to properly will send you up in flames. The brilliant English Puritan John Owen summarises this thinking like this: 'Be killing sin or it will be killing you.'[9]

The devil

The devil is always trying to trap you in sin, making good use of condemning accusation and cunning deception. Many people think he's just a cartoon character with horns, an outmoded, superstitious idea. But as Verbal, played by Kevin Spacey, said in the Academy Award–winning film *The Usual Suspects*, 'The greatest trick the devil ever pulled was convincing the world he didn't exist.' Even secular humanist Andrew Delbanco, who has been called America's best social critic, seems to agree: 'So the work of the devil is everywhere, but no one knows where to find him. We live in the most brutal century in human history, but instead of stepping forward to take credit, he has rendered himself invisible.'[10]

The Bible says Satan is a murderer and the father of lies,[11] a thief who comes to steal, kill and destroy.[12] He can disguise himself as an angel of light.[13] He prowls around like a roaring lion looking for people to devour.[14] He is the deceiver of the whole world and the condemning accuser of believers.[15]

In summary: the devil hates your guts and he wants you dead, physically and spiritually. His first appearance in the Scriptures reveals his ways of working. Please read these famous verses with fresh eyes, on the lookout for Satan's schemes:

> Now the serpent was more crafty than any other beast of the field that the Lord God had made. He said to the woman, 'Did God actually say, "You shall not eat of any tree in the garden"?' And the woman said to the serpent, 'We may eat of the fruit of the trees in the garden, but God said, "You shall not eat of the fruit of the tree that is in the midst of the garden, neither shall you touch it, lest you die."' But the serpent said to the woman, 'You will not surely die. For God knows that when you eat of it your eyes will be opened, and you will be like God, knowing good and evil.' (Gen. 3.1–5)

Satan attacks the trustworthiness of God's words, twisting them with a confusing admixture of truth and lie. God did not say 'you shall not eat of *any* tree'; he gave them *every* tree to eat from except just one. Note the attack on God's generous nature (we'll unpack that more in chapter 8). The other lie is to downplay the seriousness of sin, to say it doesn't kill. Adam and Eve didn't immediately die physically, but they did spiritually. They could no longer walk in fellowship with God in the garden as they had before. Instead, they were hiding from him in fear and shame.[16] Everything was different now.

The good news, John goes on to tell us in his letter, is that Jesus came to destroy the devil's work – that's 'the reason the Son of God appeared' (1 John 3.8). The devil has had his decisive defeat at the cross.[17] Jesus struck the definitive blow Satan cannot recover from; our total deliverance is coming, but until then we all need to get serious about playing our part in outworking Calvary's victory in our lives.

Let's recap. The war you are fighting is not against people[18] but the world, the flesh and the devil and the way they work together to ensnare, entangle and exterminate you with sin. Sin is the thing that brings them together, their weapon of mass destruction, and therefore the thing we must really get to grips with. Sin is crouching at your door to devour you like it did Cain.[19] You need to better understand it so you can fight more effectively against it, and with the weapon that the world, the flesh and the devil don't want you to wield properly: confession. You also need a solid definition of sin so you don't get lost in false guilt (for things that aren't strictly sin, like temptation). So, in the rest of this chapter, we're going to look at the definition of sin and delusions about sin, before touching on deliverance from sin.

Definition of sin

Sin is evil, full stop. It's way more contagious than COVID-19 and deadlier than the Marburg and Ebola viruses combined. If you hate what they've done to the world, you should hate sin more for the suffering it causes but especially for the treasonous, ungrateful, sticking-your-finger-up-to-God (your benevolent Creator) ugly act that it is. It is pure, concentrated poison we have no business playing around with.

The word John mostly uses for sin, *hamartia*, means 'missing the mark'. In 1 John 1.9, he also calls it unrighteousness, *adikias*, which means injustice or wrongdoing. In chapter 3 of the same letter, he says 'sin is lawlessness' – basically, living as if your ideas are superior to God's. This is what Adam and Eve did in the garden of Eden by disobeying God and eating from the tree of the knowledge of good and evil. Oxford professor John Lennox explains it brilliantly: 'To eat from the tree is to have a frame of mind that asserts the creature's will against the creator's; that pushes the creator aside and makes central to everything the pursuit of one's egotistical interests and interpretation of life. That is, in principle, what "sin" is.'[20] That's a deeper definition than most people have. Many tend to focus on sin's outer circle, legalistically obsessing about the things they can or can't do. But there is a sin beneath sin, an inner circle to it we should be more concerned about as we trace the many fruits of our sins to their corrupt common root.

The social transformer William Wilberforce once said that the majority of 'Christians' in England determined guilt 'not by the proportion in which, according to Scripture, [actions] are offensive to God, but by that in which they are injurious to society'.[21] This seems good: sin harms others, so we shouldn't do it. Right? But Wilberforce said this understanding doesn't go anything like far enough: 'Their slight notions of the guilt and evil of sin [expose] an utter want of all suitable reverence for the Divine Majesty. This principle [reverence for the Divine Majesty] is justly termed in Scripture, "The beginning of wisdom" [Ps. 111.10].'[22]

Paul, the forgiven murderer, refers to this sin beneath sin in the first chapter of his first-century letter to the Church in Rome. At its core, he says, sin is suppressing the truth about God and treasuring other things – substitutes – in his place.[23] The excellent preacher-theologian John Piper defines it well, saying sin is:

The glory of God not honored.
The holiness of God not reverenced.
The greatness of God not admired.
The power of God not praised.
The truth of God not sought.

The wisdom of God not esteemed.
The beauty of God not treasured.
The goodness of God not savored.
The faithfulness of God not trusted.
The promises of God not believed.
The commandments of God not obeyed.
The justice of God not respected.
The wrath of God not feared.
The grace of God not cherished.
The presence of God not prized.
The person of God not loved.[24]

These 'nots' are what Satan has been tempting every human being into since the beginning. They are what, as we wrote earlier in this chapter, he did to Adam and Eve in Genesis chapter 3, making them think God is bad for withholding something from them, so they would stop honouring and loving him as they should. This is how sin begins. We put terrible substitutes at the centre, in the place of the true God. They don't have the gravitational weight of deity to hold reality together, and so we get sucked into the whirlpool of many sins.

Yes, many sins. John doesn't say 'our sin' but 'our sins', plural. The record of my sins, for example, would be far, far longer, I suspect, than could be written in all the books in my local library. What about you?

Do you struggle with envy? John makes a big deal of this in his letter. Don't be like Cain, he says, who envied the favour his brother found with God and killed him.[25] Envy is distress at another's success because we want the honour. It's just one sin, but it manifests in so many ways. We get envious of others who parent better, have more athletic and attractive bodies, get better life opportunities or – worst of all for me – preach better. I'll be honest with you, attending big Bible conferences with your church can be challenging. You find yourself sitting in the main venue thinking, 'Wow, this guy preaching is great,' and then afterwards a church member says, 'That was the best sermon I've ever heard,' and you're now thinking, 'Thanks, I guess mine aren't as good as my pride would like to believe, then.' John is saying, 'Don't be like that.' Confess the sin of envy and rejoice if someone does something better than you. Please don't give them the evil eye; follow the way of love.

But maybe you're thinking, 'Envy – that's not my particular sin problem.' First, check your pride; it may be blocking you from seeing how affected by envy you actually are. Second, read the Sermon on the Mount[26] and let it search your sin out. It will ask you if you've fantasised in detail about getting revenge or getting it on with someone recently. Read through Gal. 5.19–21, work through the classic seven deadly sins or prayerfully examine your heart as you read this New Testament compilation:

Jealousy, strife, rivalries, disputes, resentment, bitterness, unforgiveness, malice, cynicism, envy, greed, coveting, ungratefulness, backstabbing, drunkenness, carousing, swindling, deceit, lying, hypocrisy, lust, fornication, sexual immorality, sexual impurity, sensuality, homosexual acts, adultery, idolatry, magical arts, occult, abuse, slander, defamation, angry outbursts, gossip, clamor, filthiness, coarse jokes, irreverence, profanity, wilfulness, impulsivity, bragging, arrogance, insolence, self-centredness, materialism, self-promotion, contempt, lack of discipline, self-indulgence, self-importance, conceit, gluttony, cowardice, unholiness.[27]

These lists will assist you to experience Holy Spirit conviction, helping you to enjoy liberating confession. Which of the sins you just read could you stop and confess right now to journey into greater joy with God?

It's important also to say what sin is not. Sin is not temptation. James said that 'desire when it has conceived gives birth to sin' (Jas.

1.15). The distinction is especially clear in Heb. 4.15, which says Jesus was 'tempted in every way, just as we are – yet he did not sin'. This is important because you may be errantly feeling guilt for things that are actually temptations. Consider lust.[28] A person addicted to viewing pornography is sinning. A man who daydreams about a woman's body is guilty of lust. But if he notices a woman is attractive but hesitates before looking and thinking longer about what he saw, he is probably in the grip of temptation and may or may not go on to commit sin. The sixteenth-century reformer Martin Luther popularised this relevant pithy proverb: 'You can't keep the birds from flying over your head but you can keep them from building a nest in your hair.'

To confess sin effectively, we must address the general root of the problem – our dishonour of God – but we also need to get specific. We need to know our own besetting sins and the characteristic ways we do wrong and fail to do right. We need to know the enticements to which we typically succumb. To help with this, we've found it useful to look at the three areas in which Satan tried to tempt Jesus, where we can succumb to sin, recorded in Luke 4.1–13. You may have read this Bible passage many times before, but we'd encourage you to read through it again now, with renewed vision, seeking God's wisdom about confession.

Note, first, that the battleground is identity. Jesus is tempted shortly after his baptism, after the Father has spoken his identity over him: 'You are my son, whom I love; with you I am well pleased' (Luke 3.22b). The first thing Satan does is to question and cast doubt about this by beginning with 'If you are the Son of God . . .' (Luke 4.3, 9). One reason Jesus is able to overcome temptation is that he never loses sight of who he really is. This is so important for Christians to understand. You cannot lose your identity as a beloved child, but you can forget who you are in Christ and become very vulnerable to sin.

We like the way Mike Breen, founder of the 3DM movement, has categorised the temptations of Jesus, and we have tried to develop and make that thinking our own to help us better identify, confess and guard against our besetting sins.[29]

Appetite – the 'I deserve it' persona

The first temptation Jesus faced was appetite: 'If you are the Son of God, command this stone to become bread' (Luke 4.3b). It is fleshly hunger for food, sex or whatever you reach for to bring you comfort that deep down you know you probably shouldn't, e.g., chocolate and pornography. It speaks of our consumerism, our instant-gratification culture that downplays negative long-term consequences. It is 'you're worth it' indulgence. King David is the bad example here. In 2 Sam. 11, it's that enjoying himself in the bedroom again rather than fighting on the battlefield. It was Adam's sin of abdication all over again. Lust begat adultery which begat murder. Bathsheba-gate.

What is your bread, that thing you crave and cave in to (even though you know it spoils and perishes and doesn't ultimately satisfy)?

Approval – the driven persona

The second temptation was approval: 'And the devil took him up and showed him all the kingdoms of the world in a moment of time, and said to him, "To you I will give all this authority and their glory, for it has been delivered to me, and I give it to whom I will. If you, then, will worship me, it will all be yours"' (Luke 4.6b–7). The devil is saying, 'Everyone will bow down to you, Jesus, if you just bow down to me. Worship me and everyone in the world will worship you.' This is about human applause, our desperate need of people's praise and affirmation – and competing against others for them – because of insecurity. It's putting being liked before pleasing God. It speaks of our celebrity culture. King Saul is the bad example here. In 1 Sam. 15, he disobeys God to please the people and builds a statue in his own honour. When confronted by Samuel (as we noted in chapter 3), he's more concerned about saving face than the offence he's committed against God.

Living for the praise of others is a huge idol in our culture, and it's hard to escape. It can dominate our thoughts and control our behaviour, from the subtleties of everyday life (I, Holly, for example, like to have my lipstick on before I face the alpha mum at the school gate) to bigger things.

In 1993, two-year-old James Bulger was murdered by Robert Thompson and Jon Venables, both only ten years old at the time. Video evidence showed them leading James away from a mall as thirty-eight people watched him being kidnapped but did nothing. A study of many tragedies like this has led to an understanding of what we now call the 'bystander effect': the more people who witness an event, the less personal responsibility each individual feels they have to do anything about it, and so the less likely it is that anyone will help.[30] Depressing, hey? But a key part is that the strength of the bystander effect on the individual is hugely determined by what they think other people think. When we put too high a value on what others think, we can even lose our very sense of what is right and wrong, and apathy ends up trumping compassion. This highlights how sins of omission can permit structural evils, like racism and sexism, to persist in society – through many of us not actively speaking out against them when we encounter them in workplaces, for example, even though we may not personally consider ourselves to be consciously racist or sexist. Approval is often the drug of choice for driven people. Accomplishment and achievement bring some applause, but it's never enough. They get angry over any sign of opposition or disloyalty. They can't cope with even a hint of criticism.

When was the last time you put pleasing people before obeying God?

Ambition – the deceitful persona

The final temptation, which often becomes sin for us, is ungodly ambition: 'And he took him to Jerusalem and set him on the pinnacle of the temple and said to him, "If you are the Son of God, throw yourself down from here, for it is written, 'He will command his angels concerning you, to guard you,' and 'On their hands they will bear you up, lest you strike your foot against a stone'" (Luke 4.9–11).

This is about avoiding three years of persevering ministry culminating in painful crucifixion. It speaks of getting known by quick means, by cutting corners, rather than hard-earned character growth. Shortcut the suffering. Why do things the hard way? Just lie, cheat and steal to get to the top – as long as you don't get caught, it's OK. A little exaggeration here, a little white lie there, what does it matter in the grand scheme of things if it means you get what you want? This speaks of our competitive culture that's all about impatience. King Absalom is the bad example here. In 2 Sam. 15, the results of David's many wives and concubines, poor fathering and weakness in dealing with Amnon's rape of Tamar fester in Absalom, Tamar's brother. He wants to prove to everyone he's better than his father. 'If only I were in charge,' you can hear him saying. He thinks he could do a better job, so he cheats his way to the top spot, but boy is he wrong. He hasn't realised how pampered and inexperienced he is compared to his dad. Get this: his first decision as 'king' results in his eventual death.

Where are you taking sinful shortcuts to get what you want, rather than growing through trial and suffering?

Identifying sin, however, isn't just an individual endeavour; it needs to be a team activity to be truly effective. We encourage you to give people you trust at the church you call home clear permission to challenge any sin they see in your life, with a spirit of gentleness.[31] Also, in our experience, regular attendance at a diverse church, where you serve alongside and open up your life to people who are not like you – of different ages, incomes and ethnicities – will help you to see your sins faster. In diverse churches you will find more people who can challenge your perspective, rattle your pride and test your patience, lovingly helping you, as you help them, to become more like Jesus through confession of sin.

Delusions about sin

There are two main delusions we want to focus on: the 'don't care' delusion and the 'despair' delusion.

Don't care

The 'don't care' or 'complacency' delusion is very common in our secular society that's downgraded sin to nonexistence, from its removal from the *Oxford Junior Dictionary*[32] to its trivialisation through association with things like 'food sins', e.g., the 'sin' of watered-down tomato ketchup or soggy chips. Now, these are bad, but such wrongness is nothing compared to sin. Our culture's approach to sin is a bit like the people most responsible for Auschwitz saying 'oops', 'whoopsie' or 'my bad' over the systematic killing of 1.1 million people. This delusion isn't new. The first-century challenge John tackled in his letter was people claiming to be without sin (1.8) and not to have sinned (1.10).

Truth be told, many of us find it hard to fully own our sins. We may be happy to talk about sin generally, in small church groups, for example – discussing this or that sin – but not often specifically and personally. It's this 'our' word John uses. We don't want to take possession of our sins and own the full horror of their rebellion, that they're far worse than a child ungratefully saying 'f— you' to his loving parent.

Doing whatever sinful thing you want has consequences, as we wrote in the Introduction. Sin and guilt are stubborn because, like gravity, they are laws of the universe that can't be sidestepped. The point is: you can't cheat sin in this life, or the next for that matter. Paul put it like this when speaking in Athens: 'In the past God overlooked such ignorance, but now he commands people everywhere to repent. For he has set a day when he will judge the world with justice by the man [Jesus] he has appointed. He has given proof of this to all men by raising him from the dead' (Acts 17.30–1 NIV). This resurrection, John said right at the start of his letter, is an historical event – he 'heard', 'looked upon' and 'touched' the risen Jesus. We need, therefore, to care very much about 'our sins'.

Despair

The 'despair' or 'crushed with hopelessness' delusion is the other end of the spectrum. Dr Martyn Lloyd-Jones called it 'that one sin' in his excellent book *Spiritual Depression*. Satan cannot rob a believer of their salvation, but he will do all he can to make them miserable. Satan means 'accuser', and one of the accusations he'll throw at you is that a particular sin you've committed is too bad, or too frequent, to be forgiven.

Lloyd-Jones tells the story of a seventy-seven-year-old man who had joyfully come to faith, only for Lloyd-Jones to find him knocking on the door of his house, dejected and weeping uncontrollably. It turned out the man had remembered something that had happened thirty years earlier. He had been drinking in a pub, arguing about religion, and had said, 'Jesus Christ was a b-----d.' It had come back to him and he felt sure there was no forgiveness for that.[33]

It's a clever strategy of the enemy because it's a subtle appeal to your pride: your sin is so special it cannot be cleansed. The truth is others will have done the very same thing, maybe worse, and been forgiven. Think about Paul. He was a blasphemer, persecutor and violent man, putting Christians to death. Yet he was not beyond the grace of God.[34] The devil, as he did with Adam and Eve, is tempting you to think less of God, when his grace all the more abounds.[35] Don't listen to Satan. Believe the promise of 1 John 1.9: if you confess, you are forgiven and cleansed from all unrighteousness, from every sin without exception.[36] Jesus will never, ever cast out *anyone* who comes to him.[37]

Sometimes I don't agree with Holly when she's right about something, from fashion faux pas to parenting fails, and it always lands me in trouble. But there is one who is even holier than my Holly, and he's always right. That's what it means to be God in the proper understanding of deity. It's impossible for him to be wrong. So are you really going to be that arrogant – relatively young, inexperienced you going up against the omnipotent, omniscient Ancient of Days? 'No, God, I think I'm right about this one sin . . . I believe it's so bad it can't be forgiven and that I should have to punish myself in some way.' That's saying, 'Your sacrifice on the cross didn't quite go far enough, God. I need to add something more so I can be forgiven. I'm right, God, and you're wrong.' Dur! We've all done it, though, haven't we? You can confess that one sin today and find forgiveness and deliverance from its power.

Deliverance from sin

When you start to own your sin, you may want to cry out like Paul did at the end of Rom. 7, 'What a wretched man that I am! Who will deliver me from this body of death?' Wonderfully, he immediately answers: 'Thanks be to God through Jesus Christ our Lord!'

Jesus, though tempted to extremes we'll never know, resisted sin so he could become sin on the cross for you. The perfect holy-human sacrifice to pay the penalty for your sin so you can be forgiven. Through faith in Jesus, you die to sin's power over you, to live in Christ's resurrection victory over it. The fourth-century theologian and transformed sex addict Augustine put it like this:

Stage 1: creation – humanity is born able to sin.
Stage 2: after the fall – humanity is not able not to sin.
Stage 3: after conversion – humanity is able not to sin.
Stage 4: after glorification – humanity is not able to sin.

You can reign over sin now, in stage three, with perhaps the greatest weapon against it: confession. Please pause to do that now. Your words don't need to be perfect to be powerful.

Questions for reflection

What is sin?

On a scale of one to ten (ten being strychnine deadly), how dangerous do you think sin is?

How do the world, flesh and the devil work to entangle *you* in sin?

What are your besetting sins?

Prayer of Confession
O Lord, Heavenly King, Comforter, Spirit of Truth, have compassion and mercy on Thy sinful servant and pardon my unworthiness, and forgive me all the sins that I humanly committed today, and not only humanly but even worse than a beast – my voluntary sins, known and unknown, from my youth and from evil suggestions, and from my brazenness, and from boredom. If I have sworn by Thy Name or blasphemed it in thought, blamed or reproached anyone, or in my anger have detracted or slandered anyone, or grieved anyone, or if I have got angry about anything, or have told a lie, if I have slept unnecessarily, or if a beggar has come to me and I despised or neglected him, or if I have troubled my brother or quarrelled with him, or if I have condemned anyone, or have boasted, or have been proud, or lost my temper with anyone, or if when standing in prayer my mind has been distracted by the glamour of this world, or if I have had depraved

thoughts or have overeaten, or have drunk excessively, or have laughed frivolously, or have thought evil, or have seen the attraction of someone and been wounded by it in my heart, or have said indecent things, or made fun of my brother's sin when my own faults are countless, or have been neglectful of prayer, or have done some other wrong that I cannot remember – for I have done all this and much more – have mercy, my Lord and Creator, on me Thy wretched and unworthy servant, and absolve and forgive and deliver me in Thy goodness and love for men, so that, lustful, sinful and wretched as I am, I may lie down and sleep and rest in peace. And I shall worship, praise and glorify Thy most honourable Name, with the Father and His only-begotten Son, now and ever, and for all ages. Amen.

Ephrem the Syrian, 306–73

Forgiveness story #5

ROBERT

I grew up in an atmosphere of underlying fear. My father wasn't ever physically violent but he could be very confrontational to others, and that destabilised me. I just didn't know whether he liked me or loved me, whether I pleased him or not. I'd overhear conversations he had which used threats of violence and would witness him responding to situations aggressively. I didn't know it then, but I was very sensitive to his outbursts and grew up fearful of most things, including relating to people well.

My dad had an extramarital affair, which crushed my mother. She internalised her feelings, which led to a long-running battle with depression. They tried to make the marriage work, but she eventually went to a hospital for treatment. The battle was to last a long time. This was devastating for someone still young. I had no one to turn to, no one to talk to about my feelings. No one even asked, as they were mostly trying to deal with their own. I realised I was completely alone. Like my mother, I internalised my feelings. I learned to cope with such negativity through fantasy and chronic masturbation. Once I started on this path, I couldn't stop. It lasted for many years.

As this habit developed, I was enticed into some shame-ridden, hidden, unhealthy relationships with other boys and girls of my age. This behaviour went on into adulthood and developed into same-sex attraction, although not exclusively. It was my big, unclean secret. On the surface, I was a regular guy, but underneath I was gradually becoming mentally unwell through living this double life. I was diagnosed with severe anxiety and mild depression. I contemplated suicide, wrote goodbye letters in my head and even found a suitable tree from which to hang myself.

Around this time, my father became a follower of Jesus and started to clean up his life. He changed. I saw him, under great provocation, turn the other cheek to an enemy. I witnessed him stopping drinking and smoking. He became lighter and more relational. He even told me he loved me. That was the clincher. I knew then that his conversion was real and not fake, as I'd once suspected. A light went on in me that changed the way I saw him, and God.

I started to dwell on eternity, on my sin before God, on my need to be saved. I was drawn to God not of myself, but by his leading. I was utterly lost in the world and had no answers of my own. I was still the afraid little boy, scared of his father, without a mother for most of his childhood. I had been searching for lost love in all the wrong places. None of them had given me what I truly wanted or, as I was to discover, needed. The result of this dwelling was a powerful realisation I didn't belong in this hidden world any longer. I'd been sensing God's invitation to follow Jesus. I called my father and he led me to church and Christ.

I decided to follow Jesus. There wasn't a clear-cut feeling of euphoria. I was still fearful and remained that way for some time to come. I lost nearly all my 'friends' at once. Although I was instantly shunned, I didn't worry about it because I'd been saved from punishment for my sins. I was given a new family and friends in God's Church. I felt lighter. I didn't feel the constant, nagging weight of guilt on my shoulders; it was gone! I was forgiven and it felt great!

This wasn't the end of my hidden struggles, though. I continued to stumble and occasionally fall. I'd go back to my old ways and return feeling condemned and completely broken. But I learned that the God of the Bible, who time and again forgave Israel when they confessed and repented of their sins, was faithful to his word. That's who he is. He delights in me in Christ. He loves me. I now see that I am a trophy of *his* grace. It's all *his* work. I still fail. I still stumble. But his love and faithfulness see me through.

5

He is faithful

'God does what he says he will do, always.'

Jen Wilkin, *In His Image*

But. Daddy. You. Said. Four words that are like nails being driven into my heart. I arrogantly thought my children would never say them. That was something that happened to other parents. I was going to be the best dad. But, like Peter promising he'd never disown Jesus,[1] it's happened, not once, or twice, or even three times. Ahh!

But it's not just me. Unfaithfulness is everywhere. Who hasn't broken their word and let someone down? It happens so often we can quantify it, at least when it comes to sexual promiscuity. Believe it or not, the nationalities, vocations and even Myers–Briggs personality profiles most likely to cheat have been ranked. There's a lot of unfaithfulness out there, but it's also in here (we type, pointing to our hearts). This is why we celebrate promises kept: marriage vows honoured for forty, fifty, sixty or eighty-six years, which is the world record, by the way . . . and stories like this: a six-foot-two, big-bearded, tattoo-covered dad wearing a 'punisher' shirt, keeping his promise to his daughter to buy clothes for her baby doll, pushing a trolley through a large shop. The event was recorded by a staff member, whose post rapidly received more than 67,000 likes because we, particularly in the political times in which we live, recognise how rare it is that promises are kept.

The problem is not just that we live in an unfaithful world but that we're tainted with unfaithfulness ourselves. As a result, we can distort God into our unfaithful image and think he's more like us than

73

his holy self. This leaves us wondering if God's promise of forgiveness in 1 John 1.9 is too good to be true. Can he really forgive me for this? Forever? Won't he change his mind? What if I sin again, in the same way, and then again – will he still forgive me then?

Buried deep within most people's psyches is the misconception that God cannot be trusted to keep his word. Now, we fall prey to all sorts of misconceptions. Like thinking you lose your body heat fastest through your head. You don't – not even if you're bald. Mount Everest is not the *tallest* mountain in the world (it's Mauna Kea in Hawaii). Vikings did not have horns on their helmets. And so on. We fall prey to all sorts of misconceptions, but don't fall prey to one of the greatest of them all: that God cannot be trusted. He can. He is 100% faithful!

Creation wonder

Christians believe God speaks through the Bible, but there's another book through which God's voice can be heard we're rather deaf to: creation. That may cause you or someone you know to stumble and even say, 'You don't really believe God created the universe, do you?' Yes, actually. We don't believe something came from nothing. To us that's more unbelievable. Science, not just the Bible, says the universe had a beginning. Sir Edwin Hubble's work and things like gravitational waves teach us that.

If the universe had a beginning, we must ask, what or who pushed the first domino? Some say, no one, it just happened. Others, like Dr Lawrence Krauss, redefine relativistic quantum fields amongst other things as 'nothing' – when they're obviously something and beg the question 'how did they get there?' Physicist Dr David Albert responded in the *New York Times* like this:

> The particular, eternally persisting, elementary physical stuff of the world, according to the standard presentations of relativistic

quantum field theories, consists (unsurprisingly) of relativistic quantum fields . . . they [Krauss et al.] have nothing whatsoever to say on the subject of where those fields came from, or of why the world should have consisted of the particular kinds of fields it does, or of why it should have consisted of fields at all, or of why there should have been a world in the first place. Period. Case closed. End of story.[2]

So, we believe the Bible's creation account. God, the uncaused spiritual being, created everything out of nothing physical . . . and he speaks through all that he has made. Paul put it like this in chapter 1 of his letter to the Church in Rome: 'For since the creation of the world God's invisible qualities – his eternal power and divine nature – have been clearly seen, being understood from what has been made, so that people are without excuse.'[3] This is a pattern throughout Scripture, like Ps. 19's wonderful beginning, 'The heavens declare the glory of God'; Solomon's encouragement to learn from ants;[4] and Jesus' anxiety management exhortation, 'Consider the lilies . . .' (Matt. 6.25–34). We're meant to hear God speaking to us through creation. Our problem is we're deaf and distracted. One of the things you'll hear if you tune in is, day after day, creation declaring God's *faithfulness*.

The Prophet Jeremiah said God is as faithful as the sun rising every day and the moon shining every night. God's faithfulness is as certain as waves rolling in and out, again and again.[5] King David, of adultery and murder fame, said in Ps. 130 that he watched for relief from God, for forgiveness, as one watched for the morning[6] – a thing that will certainly come at its appointed time. God is as faithful to forgive as the morning comes, as the sun rises, as predictable as the tides rolling in and out. Your sin is like writing in the sand of the seashore and, through confession, you can be confident that the waves of God's faithfulness will come in, wash it away and make you new again. Hallelujah! This is not so-so faithfulness or OK faithfulness, it is 'GREAT is thy faithfulness,' as Thomas Chisholm's hymn announces!

Covenant keeping

The second way we see God's faithfulness is in his covenant or promise-keeping. God makes promises to people throughout the Bible. Let's look at an early one. To infertile, elderly Abraham and Sarah, God promises 'all families of the earth will be blessed' (Gen. 12.3) through them – through the children they will have. But many painful years go by with no pregnancy. Will God deliver on his promise? Ageing Abraham is so close to giving up in Gen. 15 that he's about to let one of his servants inherit his estate, rather than having faith for his own flesh-and-blood offspring. Then God speaks again, reaffirming his promise. 'Don't look down at the weakness of your humanity,' he effectively says, 'look up.' 'Look at the stars, see my power in creation,' verse 5. 'I have the power to deliver on my promises,' God is saying.

To seal the deal they perform an ancient covenant – a contract-making ceremony. Abraham cuts a cow, a goat and a ram in half. This was expensive, time-consuming, bloody work. That's the point – a costly scene of death inviting scavengers. Usually the two parties would then shake on it and sign on the dotted line, at least in our twenty-first-century equivalent. But God appears to administer a sleeping potion to Abraham and speaks to him in a dream instead.[7] 'Know for certain that your offspring will be sojourners in a land that is not theirs . . . and will be afflicted for four hundred years' (Gen. 15.13). God promises to deliver them, though it's all a bit mysterious to say the least, but isn't that God – evidence of his holy beyond-humanness?

The point of these butchered animal carcases is to say in an unmistakable way, 'Let me become like them if I break this agreement.' By putting Abraham to sleep, God is protecting Abraham, knowing he would be unfaithful to his part of the contract – obediently trusting God and taking possession of all that God had promised. So, God alone walks through the carcases, in (inviting and terrifying) smoke and fire, in holy glory, saying, 'Let this curse fall on me if this agreement is broken.' The rest of the biblical story is God keeping his promise. In Exod. chapters 6–14, God delivers the Israelites after 430 years of slavery. God keeps his part of the covenant again and again, even when Israel keeps breaking it. Only a few chapters later, at Mount Sinai, they begin to worship false gods again.

Ps. 78 NIV summarises Israel's – and our relationship – with God well. Verse 8: 'whose spirit was not faithful to God'. Verse 17: 'Yet they sinned still more against him, rebelling against the Most High in the desert,' ungratefully demanding their Egyptian slave diet again. Verses 23–4: 'Yet he [God] commanded the skies above . . . he rained down on them manna to eat and gave them the grain of heaven.' Verse 27: 'He rained meat on them like dust.' Verse 32: 'In spite of all this, they still sinned; despite his wonders, they did not believe.' Verse 37: 'Their heart was not steadfast toward him or loyal to him; they were not faithful to his covenant.' Verse 38: 'Yet he was merciful; he forgave their iniquities and did not destroy them . . .'

This continues right up to the cross and the resurrection of Jesus. It's particularly clear in chapter 22 of Luke's first-century biography, recording the Last Supper, which connects us right back to the events of Gen. 15. Jesus took the bread, gave thanks, broke it in half just like those cut-up animals, and said, 'This is my body, which is given for you. Do this in remembrance of me.' When he took the cup he said, 'This cup that is poured out for you is the *new covenant* in my blood.' God is saying, 'This is how I will make good on my promise to deliver you from sin, by being butchered myself on the most brutal form of execution known in the first century: the cross.'

God takes the just wrath for your unfaithfulness, your contract-breaking, your sin, on himself. Jesus was faithful to his dying breath to purchase your salvation and remains just as faithful in resurrection glory, promising to build his Church. Empires have fallen. Companies have disappeared. Predictions have been made about the Church's demise, down through the centuries by Enlightenment intellectuals like Voltaire,[8] but the Church still stands. And she's not just surviving, she's thriving. Of the world's population, 31% claim to be Christian today.[9]

Confident confession

This means you can trust God to forgive you when you confess, every time you confess, for whatever you confess. 'He who calls you is faithful; he will surely do it' (1 Thess. 5.24). '[H]e cannot deny himself' (2 Tim. 2.13b). His Godness demands he be faithful to his promise to forgive you and cleanse you from all – yes, all – unrighteousness (including your unfaithfulness). As the wonderful Christian writer Jen Wilkin puts it: 'God does what he says he will do, always. Those he saves, he is able to save to the uttermost, so complete is his faithfulness. He is faithful to his children because he cannot be unfaithful to himself. He is incapable of infidelity on any level.'[10]

God, remarkably, has built our unfaithfulness, as he did with Abraham, into our relationship with him. He doesn't expect you to be perfect. But that doesn't mean you just fall asleep like Abraham and let God do all the work. God does do all the heavy lifting in salvation, but you still have a part to play in your sanctification. We are to cooperate with him, confess and respond rightly to his faithfulness by being faithful. God's loving faithfulness to you will empower you to be faithful to him. Perhaps this analogy will help. My beautiful wife gets chatted up by younger men than me. Worse, they're better looking and seemingly more successful than this ageing, somewhat grumpy church leader with a less impressive salary. You're right, I shouldn't let her out of my sight. But here's the thing – she brushes off their advances because she made a promise to me, before God, that she intends to keep. The point is, her faithful love awakens faithful love in me. Holly's faithfulness keeping her marriage promises to me, in spite of all my failings, motivates me to keep my promises to her, to love her even more.

How much more so should this be with God? He said no to sin, to temptation the likes of which we can't even imagine because we quickly cave in, so he could save you in the cutting of a new covenant at the cross, by willingly being cut up himself. Oh, how that should make us want to be faithful to him – to have no other lovers, sinful idols of comfort, image, reputation and suchlike, before him. God is inviting you to live in his faithfulness and to live out his faithfulness today – to confess with confidence, certain he will forgive.

Questions for reflection

How faithful are you?

What is creation saying, if you're listening, about God's faithfulness?

What does the biblical narrative teach about God's faithfulness?

How should knowing the lengths to which God will go to keep his promises give you courage to confess your sins?

Prayer of Confession
As I rise from sleep I thank Thee, O Holy Trinity, for
through Thy great goodness and patience Thou wast
not angered with me, an idler and sinner, nor hast Thou
destroyed me in my sins, but hast shown Thy usual love for
men, and when I was prostrate in despair, Thou hast raised
me to keep the morning watch and glorify Thy power.
And now enlighten my mind's eye and open my mouth
to study Thy words and understand Thy commandments
and do Thy will and sing to Thee in heartfelt adoration and
praise Thy Most Holy Name of Father, Son and Holy Spirit,
now and ever, and to the ages of ages. Amen.

Basil the Great, 330–79

Forgiveness story #6

MAEGAN

I had built up quite a reputation as the person to go to for a Tarot card reading or reiki healing. That was the 'New Age' world I was into, even to the point of having 'angel wings' tattooed on my wrist as a sign of my commitment to my 'guides'. I didn't think I (or my daughter, whom I was raising on my own) needed God; I had my faith rooted in the spiritual realm of the occult. That's why I resisted my parents' and nephew's encouragement to try church. But because of their persistent badgering, I felt like I had to go once. 'Just once,' I thought, 'then they'll leave me alone.' Only my daughter and I were both deeply moved by the service and wanted to go back. We kept going until we independently responded to an invitation the church leader made to put our trust in Jesus. We wanted to follow Jesus but neither of us knew exactly what that meant.

Some weeks later, I was challenged by Scriptures I was given, about not practising astrology or worshipping the sun, moon, stars or angels. A wave of conviction came over me. It wasn't heavy. It was a gentle opening of my eyes that this was wrong. I was compelled not just to confess this sin but to clear out hundreds of crystals, Tarot card decks, Buddha statues and all sorts of occultic divination paraphernalia, thousands of pounds' worth of stuff. I crushed them all into a wheelie bin, so they'd be taken out of circulation and destroyed. I even began to receive treatment to remove that tattoo. I felt liberated, closer to God and lighter in my spirit.

As I began to grow in my faith, I became more aware of other areas of sin. God has dealt so graciously with me. Instead of hitting me with all my sins at once, he's drawn my conscience to them one by one and gently shown me that I need to turn away from them, and as I've confessed them, he has set me free from their shame. I say 'shame' because it was the feeling of being dirty, worthless and not good enough that kept taking residence inside me. I just couldn't see how I could ever be good enough to be used by God. But as I kept confessing my sins to God, in the presence of a mature Christian, the shame fell away. It's been such a freeing experience. Grace has been poured into my heart in this experience of total forgiveness. In it, I have found the strength to do what was impossible in the past, to forgive my daughter's father, my former partner – and to bless him.

6
And just

'I have no words, no meaning, no life, no hope if there is not a God of history and time who is absolutely outraged, absolutely furious, absolutely burning with anger toward those who took it into their own hands to commit such acts.'
                              Gary Haugen, *Good News About Injustice*

#Blacklivesmatter protesters, following the brutal murder of George Floyd, understandably outraged, marched in massive numbers just two streets away from where we live. Many were carrying signs calling for justice. We believe they were saying racism is absolutely wrong everywhere, for everyone. We agree. There were no equivocations or caveats in what they were demanding. This presumes, as we touched on in the Introduction, the existence of a transcendent morality binding on people of every creed and colour, an existential 'should' written on our hearts; it presumes that, in the words of C.S. Lewis, we 'ought to behave in a certain way, and cannot really get rid of it'.[1]

Despair

Without this holy standard, there is no hope for justice, nothing with which we can legitimately call people to account. Without God, there is no one we can trust to administer justice with moral perfection. Our lives become, in the words Arthur Miller put on the lips of one of his characters in the play *After the Fall*, an 'endless argument with oneself – this pointless litigation of existence before an empty bench. Which, of course, is another way of saying – despair'.[2]

This is the tragic outcome of a worldview that discards God. In the words of one of the high priests of atheism, Richard Dawkins: 'In a universe of electrons and selfish genes, blind physical forces and genetic replication, some people are going to get hurt, other people are going to get lucky, and you won't find any rhyme or reason in it, nor any justice. The universe that we observe has precisely the properties we should expect if there is, at bottom, no design, no purpose, no evil, no good, nothing but blind, pitiless indifference.'[3] Read those words again: 'nor *any* justice . . . nothing but blind, pitiless *indifference*'. Despair indeed.

I was fifteen when the genocide in Rwanda took place. It barely registered in my busy, self-absorbed life. It wasn't until 2001, when I visited Rwanda with a team of trainees and young lawyers, that I began to try to wrap my head around what had taken place: 800,000 people murdered in 100 days, sometimes by their next-door neighbours, using machetes. After this first visit to Rwanda I did some research. I went to my local library to look at microfiche of newspapers from April and May 1994. It was nothing but a footnote, not even a front-page headline. The only thing noticeable in the minimal coverage it got was the world's unwillingness to call what was taking place genocide. That would have required action to be taken, and with the troubles in Bosnia, and the Black Hawk Down incident fresh in people's memories, there was no stomach for stories of Western soldiers dying overseas, dare I say it, for black people.

An unsung hero amidst this atrocity, General Roméo Dallaire, leading a UN peacekeeping force in Rwanda at the time, was left completely unsupported. He was refused permission to do anything to stop the bloodshed. The world stood by, myself included, carrying on with our daily lives, and did pretty much nothing.

Is there any hope in this story of despair?

Yes. It comes in part from Gary Haugen. His experience as a lawyer serving in the aftermath stirred him to establish the brilliant

International Justice Mission. This quote, from his book *Good News About Injustice*, so moved me I memorised it:

> the knowledge of God's great anger toward and condemnation of injustice is what gives me hope to seek justice in this world. Standing with my boots knee-deep in the reeking muck of a Rwandan mass grave, where thousands of innocent people have been horribly slaughtered, I have no words, no meaning, no life, no hope if there is not a God of history and time who is absolutely outraged, absolutely furious, absolutely burning with anger toward those who took it into their own hands to commit such acts.[4]

The bench is not empty

The foundations of reality and our common-sense experience of them reveal that the bench is *not* empty. For example, have you ever sat on a train at a station with another train on a track next to you, unsure whether you or the adjacent train is moving? What did you do? In that situation, we look for a reference point independent of ourselves, like a lamppost or a tree, an absolute object by which we can determine whether or not the train we're on is moving. This is what we do when we say something is right or wrong, in a way that goes beyond personal (subjective) opinion. We look for an absolute standard by which to judge. In other words, every cry for justice is a conscious or subconscious call upon the judge of all the earth[5] – God – to do right. Note: if God doesn't act in just judgement, he's doing wrong.

History also points to the origins of the just society we aspire to today. Award-winning historian and writer Tom Holland says in the top-selling book *Dominion*:

> That every human being possessed an equal dignity was not a remotely self-evident truth. A Roman would have laughed at it.

To campaign against discrimination on the grounds of gender, or sexuality, however, was to depend on large numbers of people sharing a common assumption: that everyone possessed an inherent worth. The origins of this principle – as Nietzsche had so contemptuously pointed out – lay not in the French Revolution, nor in the Declaration of Independence, nor in the Enlightenment, but in the Bible.[6]

The bench is not empty; God has revealed his just character in history and Scripture. He heard the lament of his own people's suffering in Egypt and took action to rescue them.[7] He heard the cries of injustice against his people and intervened, first with the Assyrians, then the Babylonians; he judged and exiled them. He hears the cry of the downtrodden today and calls his people to 'seek justice' (Isa. 1.17) for them; this is the 'religion that is pure and undefiled before God' (Jas. 1.27) that pleases him. The Mosaic law,[8] the role of the prophet[9] and the purpose of kingship[10] all work for justice, but nowhere do we see God's heart for justice more clearly than at the cross. This is beautifully described by William Rees in the hymn 'Here Is Love':

> On the Mount of Crucifixion fountains opened
> deep and wide;
> Through the floodgates of God's mercy flowed a
> vast and gracious tide.
> Grace and love like mighty rivers poured
> incessant from above,
> And heaven's peace and perfect justice kissed a guilty
> world in love.

God is so committed to justice he's willing to die for it. He experienced the greatest injustice of all as the ultimate innocent one sentenced to death, dying to defeat sin and deliver on his promise of forgiveness. This is how God answers perhaps the greatest of all riddles, 'how can he be loving (forgive) and just (punish) – at the *same* time?' By paying the ultimate penalty himself.

This also means forgiveness isn't a whimsical decision God will change his mind about. It's written in blood by an unchangeable act. God has orchestrated all of this to give you absolute assurance of his forgiveness.

An advocate with the father

This is what John goes on to write about in chapter 2 of his letter: 'But if anyone does sin, we have an *advocate* with the Father, Jesus Christ the righteous. He is the propitiation for our sins, and not for ours only but also for the sins of the whole world' (1 John 2.1b–2).[11]

I used to be an advocate, what we call in England a criminal barrister. We were taught to be the mouthpieces for our clients, paid to argue the merits of the case to the best of our ability. Whatever I achieved, my client achieved. Think Russian dolls. Theologian Charles Hodge described the relationship eloquently: 'The client does not appear. He is not heard. He is not regarded. He is lost in his advocate, who for the time being is his representative.' Then he applies this to the Christian faith: 'This is the relation in which Christ as our advocate stands to us. He appears before God for us. We are lost in him. He, not we, is seen, heard, and regarded. It is not necessary that the client be personally present. His advocate supplies his place. Christ thus assumes our position.'[12]

It's interesting also what John didn't say. Outstanding New York pastor Tim Keller helped us to see this.[13] It's not Jesus Christ the merciful or the persuasive, but 'the righteous'. A really good lawyer doesn't just play on the emotions of the court, unless he has been landed with a terrible case. In the profession we used to call that 'making bricks without straw' and it was always embarrassing. Jesus has a great case, but what is it? It is 'the propitiation [or atoning sacrifice] for our sins'. Propitiation is the nullification of sin through a wrath-absorbing sacrifice that appeases the demands of holy justice. Jesus' case is the justice of the cross. Jesus isn't pleading for forgiveness before the Father, he's pleading his own perfect righteousness – the sufficiency of his sacrificial death. He's faithfully, continually, always[14] saying something like: 'Father, yes [insert your name here] did do it again but I have died the death she/he should have died and have lived the life she/he should have lived in her/his place. I am her/his advocate. She/he is lost in me. It would be unjust for you to take another payment for this sin. I have paid for it in full. I do not therefore ask for mercy, I demand justice.'

Please don't misunderstand – it's not that the Father needs persuading. It's that you do! This figurative representation of what's going on in the heavenly courtroom is designed by God to give you an ever-flowing source of consolation. It's not just the faithfulness of God but the justice of God that guarantees your acquittal, again and again and again. This is love! That same phrase 'the propitiation [or atoning sacrifice] for our sins' occurs in 1 John 4.10. It is immediately followed by 'Beloved' – that's your identity, by the way – 'if God so loved us, we also ought to love one another' (1 John 4.11). Not just loved but *so* – SO – loved. Breathe it in deep. The justice of God demands forgiveness for people who put their faith in Christ. And those who have been forgiven much love much,[15] which includes seeking justice for the oppressed. Or, in the words of the prophet Micah (6.8), 'do justice . . . love kindness . . . walk humbly with your God'. Which arguably is another way of saying 'walk in the light' (1 John 1.7).

Questions for reflection

What is the ultimate expression of God's justice? Why?

What is the significance of Jesus being our advocate?

How should God's justice give a believer assurance of forgiveness?

How does being forgiven much help you to love much?

Prayer of Confession

O Lord, who hast mercy upon all, take away from me my
sins, and mercifully kindle in me the fire of Thy Holy Spirit.
Take away from me the heart of stone, and give me a heart
of flesh, a heart to love and adore Thee, a heart to delight in
Thee, to follow and to enjoy Thee, for Christ's sake. Amen.

Ambrose of Milan, *c.* 340–397

Forgiveness story #7

PHIL

For the first twenty or so years of my life, I arrogantly thought I was a good person because I wasn't a stereotypically immoral one. Partly as a result of the Christian setting I grew up in, I learned to earn God's approval by the quality of the life I lived.

One day, secretly frustrated by the emptiness of this performance-based existence, I reflected deeply on Jesus' parable of the prodigal son in Luke 15.11–32. Having always seen myself as a better version of the younger brother, I suddenly realised I was the just-as-lost elder brother in the story, so proud in his performance.

It was a major shock, tinged with great sadness. I was so near to God, yet so far from him. I'd discovered I didn't really know God, his unconditional love and acceptance. I'd even been pushing him away. I didn't have a good understanding of sin. I thought it was just about not doing bad things, but the sin in my heart was about trying to be good enough for God. I saw just how terribly self-righteous I was and felt utterly lost.

It was also a massive relief. This son, who was full of self-righteous religion, was still invited by the father to come in and enjoy the celebration. I was suddenly lost but also sweetly found. The runaway son's transforming embrace was also mine. God had freely forgiven me. For the first time, I think I really tasted forgiveness – it made me truly hungry for God and deeply thankful for his mercy.

I learned that day to identify and confess the sin beneath sin, not just wrongful external behaviours but also their ugly internal drivers. This has brought me so much closer to God. I am becoming more sensitive to his Holy Spirit conviction as he continues to save me from being a very religious man and I learn to abide in his loving acceptance.

7

To forgive us our sins

'Even as the angry, vengeful thoughts boiled through me, I
saw the sin of them. Jesus Christ had died for this man; was
I going to ask for more? *Lord Jesus*, I prayed, *forgive me and
help me to forgive him . . .*'

Corrie ten Boom, *The Hiding Place*

Running, whilst somehow also leaping and dancing, with out-
stretched arms and tear-filled eyes, she charged to embrace her
family after twenty-one years in prison. This is the true story of
sixty-four-year-old Alice Johnson, celebrating freedom for the first
time after her life sentence for a drugs crime (to which she admitted
guilt) was commuted by the US president.

This wonderful earthly picture of forgiveness is, however, only
a distant shadow of its heavenly counterpart. Her criminal record
remains – in databases and on Google. Through confession as
described in 1 John 1.9, however, God sends the legal guilt of your sins
away, that feeling of rottenness, to a place of no remembrance that cannot be reached, from which it is not possible to return. It's extremely
important you know what many Christians are yet to fully grasp –
what actually happens to sins when God forgives them. In Scripture,
he has graciously given all sorts of images to help you understand just
how generous his forgiveness is, so you can live in joyful freedom.

Sent away

Let's start with the meaning of the word 'forgive' in 1 John 1.9,
aphiemi, to 'leave' or 'send away'. It connects with the scapegoat

practice from the book of Leviticus.¹ Sins were confessed by the high priest onto a goat that was then sent out into the wilderness, never to return. Gone. Forever. That's the point.

Lifted off

The aching pain of King David's adulterous guilt that led to murder was, Ps. 32.1 reports, lifted off him; that's the literal meaning behind the Hebrew word translated 'forgiven'. The same is described for Christian in John Bunyan's *Pilgrim's Progress* – as he came to the cross, the crushing, exhausting burden on his shoulders was lifted off, fell down, tumbled down the hill and disappeared into an empty tomb, where he 'saw it no more'.[2]

Covered

Ps. 32.1 continues: 'whose sin is *covered*'. Paul picks up on this in Rom. 4.7–8. God hides your sins from view. Instead of seeing wickedness, he sees righteousness, the robe he adorns every believer with – garments of praise instead of despair.[3]

Removed

God removes and takes away your sins. Ps. 103.12 says: 'As far as the east is from the west, so far does he remove our transgressions from us'. That's not even a really, really long way to travel. It is infinitely far away – that's the point – impossible to reach or come back from. John the Baptist said it like this: 'Behold, the Lamb of God, who *takes away* the sin of the world!' (John 1.29).[4]

Blotted out

According to Isa. 43.25 and 44.22, sin is 'blotted out'. It is erased from the record, deleted. It is as if it never existed. In New Testament Pauline language, your record of debt has been *cancelled*.[5]

Un-remembered[6]

At least four times[7] in speaking of forgiveness, God says he will re-member your sins no more. *I* will not remember. I *will* not remember. I will *not* remember. I will not *remember*. 'What sins are you talking about . . .?' God says after you've confessed them.

Trampled underfoot

The prophet Micah said God treads your sins underfoot.[8] His pestle-and-mortar forgiveness grinds them down so small as to barely even exist, crushed to dust. Think also how Jesus, fulfilling Gen. 3.15, stamped on Satan's head with his nail-pierced feet, silencing the great accuser forever. 'There is therefore now no condemnation for those who are in Christ Jesus' (Rom. 8.1).

Cast into the depths

Micah continues to say he will 'cast all our sins into the depths of the sea' (Mic. 7.19). God drowns your sins. Again, he sends them to a place from which it's impossible to return. Consider the Egyptians chasing after the people of God through the Red Sea during the Ex-odus, only to be swallowed up as the waters of judgement engulfed them.[9] Israel's sinful past (idolatry in Egypt) was not meant to travel with them into their promised-land future; neither is yours!

When you confess your sins God sends them away, he lifts them off, he covers them, he removes them, he blots them out, he un-remembers them, he tramples them underfoot and he casts them into the depths of the sea. Gone. Gone. Gone. Don't let them live on! Believe what God says about them.

Jesus is the true and better scapegoat. The sin of the world was laid on him as he was sent out. He willingly became the ultimate outsider so you can joyfully be the ultimate insider. In Christ, you are *forgiven*! God sees you as holy. Now live that way. How? One obvious application is to forgive others, as Christ has forgiven you. In fact, holding on to bitterness will keep you in a prison of unforgiveness. Reminder: it is the first sin in Paul's Eph. 4.31 list that follows grieving the Holy Spirit. Is its poison pulsing through your veins? Get rid of it by confessing it now.

At South Africa's Truth and Reconciliation Commission, it's said a policeman named van de Broek recounted how he and other officers shot an eighteen-year-old boy and burned the body.[10] Then, eight years later, he returned, seized the boy's father, and forced the man's wife to watch her husband be burned alive. Silence. A holy hush is said to have fallen in that courtroom as the elderly woman who had lost both son and husband was asked, 'What do you want from Mr van de Broek?'

First, she asked for a decent burial for them from the dust where they had died. His head down, the policeman nodded in agreement. Second, she said, 'Mr van de Broek took all my family away from me, and I still have a lot of love to give. Twice a month, I would like for him to come to the township and spend a day with me so I can be a mother to him. And I would like Mr van de Broek to know that he is forgiven by God and that I forgive him too. I would like to embrace him so he can know my forgiveness is real.'

Some in the courtroom spontaneously began to sing 'Amazing Grace' but van de Broek could not hear the hymn. He had fainted, overwhelmed. The forgiveness you receive from God is so much greater. It should overwhelm you. Then once you come round, it should stir you not just to uproot your sin, confessing your unforgiveness, but to sow righteousness, loving others by forgiving them.

The amazing Corrie ten Boom, coming face to face with one of her SS concentration camp jailers, powerfully illustrates how:

Even as the angry, vengeful thoughts boiled through me, I saw the sin of them. Jesus Christ had died for this man; was I going to ask for more? *Lord Jesus*, I prayed, *forgive me and help me to forgive him*. I tried to smile, I struggled to raise my hand. I could not. I felt nothing, not the slightest spark of warmth or charity. And so again I breathed a silent prayer. *Jesus, I cannot forgive him. Give Your forgiveness.* As I took his hand the most incredible thing happened. From my shoulder along my arm and through my hand, a current seemed to pass from me to him, while into my heart sprang a love for this stranger that almost overwhelmed me. And so I discovered that it is not on our forgiveness any more than on our goodness that the world's healing hinges, but on His. When He tells us to love our enemies, He gives, along with the command, the love itself.[11]

The persecuted Church provides many moving stories to inspire us to forgive. We have so much to learn from the people affected, like Jeovani, a teenager in the Central African Republic. The brilliant Open Doors charity[12] reports he was sitting in church when a grenade exploded at his feet. It was thrown into the building by a group of Islamic extremists. Jeovani's legs had to be amputated. He had to learn to walk with sticks before the hospital gave him artificial legs. He may never run again. His approach towards his attackers, though, is extraordinary: 'If I should one day meet the Muslim man who shot the grenades at my church, I will not be angry. I will smile. I do not even have the heart to hurt him. I think that he doesn't really know how terrible it is what he has done. I will greet him and say, "God forgives you, and He wants me to forgive you too. You do not know what you have done to me, but I forgive you." And once I have told him that, I will never be angry with him.'[13]

Questions for reflection

What image of forgiveness most impacts you? Do you believe it?

Whom, and for what, do you need to forgive?

Prayer of Confession
ALMIGHTY and most merciful Father; We have erred, and strayed from thy ways like lost sheep. We have followed too much the devices and desires of our own hearts. We have offended against thy holy laws. We have left undone those things which we ought to have done; And we have done those things which we ought not to have done; And there is no health in us. But thou, O Lord, have mercy upon us, miserable offenders. Spare thou those, O God, who confess their faults. Restore thou those who are penitent; According to thy promises declared unto mankind In Christ Jesus our Lord. And grant, O most merciful Father, for his sake; That we may hereafter live a godly, righteous, and sober life, To the glory of thy holy Name. Amen.
The Book of Common Prayer, Daily Office:
Morning/Evening Prayer, 1662

Forgiveness story #8

TANIA

I was raised in an atheist home. My parents separated when I was very young. Even though thankfully my sister and I remained close to both our mum and dad and we had a wonderful, loving extended family, something was missing. I saw in a wealthy aunt that her money brought no lasting joy. Most relationships around me, be they with family, friends or acquaintances, were far from perfect. In school, I was part of the 'cool crew', but to keep up with whatever fad there was in various friendship factions, I ended up entangling myself in all sorts of shameful gossip and lies. I remember, when I was in my early teens, lying in bed unable to get to sleep, worried about what my so-called friends thought of me and at times scared about the consequences of my scheming. I had a restless mind and a heavy heart.

Around that time, my older sister became a Christian. The radical transformation of her life and the inexplicable joy I saw in her made me want to find out more. I vividly remember the evening I prayed a very simple prayer acknowledging my sinfulness and inviting Jesus into my heart. That simple confession, consisting of a few sentences, remarkably lifted the heavy burden of worry and fear I'd been feeling. It untangled me from the webs of lies and gossip. I felt free. I felt joy like I'd never felt before.

Yes, I lost some of my 'friends', but somehow I was no longer concerned about my reputation and being popular. Since then, over the past twenty years, my Christian walk has gone through many different seasons, seasons of growth and thriving, seasons of doubt and stagnation, and also seasons of rebellion and backsliding. In all of those seasons, I ended up in a place of needing to seek God's forgiveness afresh for 'small' things and also for things that I could never have imagined I was capable of doing. Every time I confessed, the burden was lifted. When I look back away from myself to the loving hands of God that have held me, lifted me and guided me over the years and continue to do so, I see nothing but a trail of undeserved mercy and unfailing, forgiving love.

8

And

'The kingdom that Jesus preached and lived was all about a glorious, uproarious, absurd generosity.'

Tom Wright, *Luke for Everyone*

Have you ever been misjudged? It isn't nice, is it? Perhaps, like us, you've had people question your motives and say or think terrible things about you that aren't true.

A few years back there was a more humorous incident when I took Holly clothes shopping with vouchers bought for her birthday. Just so you know, I feel awkward the moment I walk into a shop that only sells women's clothes. Holly chose some dresses and asked a sales assistant where to try them on. The assistant took us into the changing area, a fancy place in the middle of the store, and told me to sit on a sofa in the centre, surrounded by curtain-covered cubicles. Whilst Holly tried on the clothes, I began to think about how I would answer the difficult 'does it suit me?' questions that were coming. After a short time, another member of staff walked in, maybe the manager, and in a shocked, shrill voice she shouted, 'What do you think you're doing here? Men can't sit here, it's completely inappropriate . . .' Treating me like a sexual predator, she marched me out to stand in the corner of the shop before I could fully explain. I had to stay there under her beady, judgemental eye for some time, until Holly came to rescue me.

Being misjudged isn't nice, but this is how we treat God. Too often we default to seeing him as the indifferent dad or mean man upstairs rather than the generous host of the universe. Perhaps the Church is partly responsible for this; do our lives give sufficient testimony to the incredible generosity of God? But then there's also been a campaign to discredit God from the beginning, which can cause you to lose confidence in his willingness to generously forgive. The 'and' God of not just addition but multiplication – that's the topic we're going to explore in this chapter; the God who does immeasurably more than we ask or even imagine.[1]

The good start

In the beginning, God created the universe.[2] We're not persuaded that something, the universe, came out of nothing, as we wrote in chapter 5. No, God, the uncaused cause, created out of nothing physical.

The Bible begins with the generous creativity of God. In its very first chapter, the words 'given', 'all' and 'every' are prominent and repeated. Gen. 1.29b–30: 'I have *given* you *every* plant yielding seed that is on the face of *all* the earth, and *every* tree with seed in its fruit. You shall have them for food. And to *every* beast of the earth and to *every* bird of the heavens and to *everything* that creeps on the earth, *everything* that has the breath of life, I have *given every* green plant for food.'

God created a diverse paradise teeming with life for humanity to live in and enjoy. He put people in it who most certainly hadn't earned the right to be there and gave them everything they needed to flourish. *And* it was good. This is what God is like, and what we are most meant to know about him from the first words of scriptural revelation.

The richest person in the world, at the time of writing, is Jeff Bezos, amongst other things Amazon.com CEO.[3] His net worth is currently $197 billion. He is more than twice as rich as the British monarchy. He makes $2,537 per second. He is so rich that in terms of proportion of net worth, the average American spending $1 is equivalent to Bezos spending $1.95 million. But he is practically destitute compared to God. God has infinite riches because he can create *ex nihilo*, out of nothing, whatever and whenever he wants, and everything, including Bezos' billions, belongs to him, and he can call the loan in any time he chooses. *And* God doesn't hoard his wealth like Bezos and so many of us, giving only a small percentage. God gives generously again and again and again. That's the message of creation, and Christ's coming, as we shall see. But the problem is, we find it hard to fully grasp this generosity because of the Great Deception.

The Great Deception

We're not talking about the false claim popularised by a disgraced televangelist that drinking silver can help kill the coronavirus. Terrible though that was, we're talking about a deception at least a billion times worse: the lies the serpent Satan spoke in Gen. 3 that persist today. Central to Satan's strategy is to attack God's character and make him seem mean. So when we believe those lies, we become mean ourselves.

Satan says, 'Did God actually say, "You shall not eat of *any* tree in the garden"?' and 'You will not surely die. For God knows when you eat of it your eyes will be opened, and you will be like God . . .'[4] Satan attacks God's generosity. He makes out God as a killjoy, who prohibited eating from any tree rather than just one. He suggests God is mean because he's withholding this one thing from you, a suggestion that stops you from seeing everything else God has already given you. Have you noticed how you often fixate on what you don't have? Some people so chase after the career success they don't yet have that they lose sight of the loving partner and children at home they've already been given.

This fixation on what you don't have can result in you living with a scarcity mindset, thinking there won't be enough and that you need to 'take and eat' everything you can, as soon as you can, because you're in competition with others. You can't trust God to give you what you need, so you have to take it for yourself. Everything is scarce, especially your time, so you have to jockey for position to get on the train or ensure you're in the fastest queue where you buy your lunch. Another word to describe this living for yourself is 'sin'.

The glorious unveiling[5]

God gives himself to destroy this Great Deception – the ultimate Christmas gift, Jesus, the baby wrapped in cloths in a manger. Jesus grows up to perform extravagantly generous miracles, starting with his first at the wedding in Cana.[6] Announcing what God is like, he has six stone jars filled, holding 20–30 gallons of water, and turns that water into top-notch Châteaux Margaux wine. (Maybe not Châteaux Margaux, but it does say the best wine was saved for last.) This works out as 600–1,000 bottles of joy-facilitating, quality wine. At our wedding, we only had twenty!

The other miracles tell the same story. Jesus helps fishermen catch dozens and dozens of fish, not once[7] but twice, 153 of them on one occasion.[8] He miraculously feeds 5,000 men, 15,000 including women and children. He does it so abundantly there are twelve baskets full of leftovers.[9] When a paralysed man is brought before him, he doesn't just heal him, he forgives his sins as well.[10] He is the *and* God offering healing and forgiveness.

The same generosity is seen in Jesus' parables. A God-like king who allows a debt equivalent to 200,000 years of income to accrue and forgives it all.[11] A vineyard owner who pays people far more than he should, when they haven't even worked a whole day.[12] A king who sends wedding invitations for an amazing banquet to every undesirable person in the vicinity.[13] A Good Samaritan who doesn't just stop to help an injured man who is his ethnic enemy, he binds up his wounds. More, he risks his life, like a Native American heading into Dodge City with an unconscious cowboy on his horse[14] – he takes him to an inn and pays for his stay.[15] *And* a father who gives away half his estate to a rebellious son who wants him dead – and when the son returns having wasted it all, doesn't just take him back as a servant but gives him a robe, ring and sandals (authority and trust) and holds a feast to honour his return.[16]

God is so generous that, in our humanity, we question whether it's right. Shouldn't that son be punished? Isn't it wrong to pay people who worked eight hours the same wage as those who worked just one? But God isn't human. His supply cannot run out! And it's his choice to be generous with what he has.

Jesus' miracles are generous, his parables are generous, and so is the content of his teaching. He speaks of turning the other cheek.[17] Giving your cloak away as well as your tunic.[18] Going the extra mile.[19] And loving even your enemies.[20] 'The kingdom that Jesus preached and lived,' world-renowned Bible scholar Tom Wright says, 'was all about a glorious, uproarious, absurd generosity.'[21]

Jesus lived and died with this kind of generosity. We became enemies of God but Jesus chose the agony of dying on a cross to show us true love, defeating sin and all the evil powers against us. 'For God so loved the world,' John wrote, 'that he *gave* his only Son, that whoever believes in him should not perish but have eternal life.'[22]

God's generosity is different from humanity's. We give our leftovers to good causes. God gives his everything to his enemies, rebellious sinners. Through faith in Christ, you have been blessed, not with a few or even many but with '*every* spiritual blessing in the heavenly places'.[23]

He doesn't just take away your sin at the cross. He gives you the power to live without sin through the resurrection. It's justification *and* sanctification, being given a righteousness not your own *and* Holy Spirit *resurrection* power to live a transformed life.

The Roman historian Tacitus said Christianity was 'checked for a moment' by Jesus' crucifixion only to break 'out afresh not only in Judea, the first source of the evil,[24] but also in the city of Rome'. This was where Christians, called a 'class' and an 'immense multitude', were persecuted, 'torn by dogs', 'nailed to crosses' and burned alive as torches.[25] That's rapid Church growth being reported, by a reliable witness, close in time to the events. In spite of the death of the founder (which normally kills off a movement), Christianity didn't just survive, it thrived. The Christian faith travelled hundreds of miles from its humble origins, roughly the same distance from the Shetland Islands (north of Scotland) to Rome, in a matter of decades, before planes, trains and automobiles and in a climate of persecution. Jesus' resurrection gave his followers the courage to live cross-shaped lives, to live boldly without fear because they knew the One who had triumphed over the penalty of sin, death.

God doesn't leave a job unfinished. He's not like some dodgy rogue-trading builder. God completes what he starts.[26] He deals with the guilt of sin *and* the stain of sin. He forgives sin *and* cleanses you from it (as we'll see in the next chapter). He puts you right *and* gives you the power to live right.

We often don't get to experience all of that, though, because 'we do not ask' (Jas. 4.2). We think God is not generous enough to forgive us our sins because they are too big, or too small, or too often repeated. So we don't experience the fullness of his forgiveness. Or if we do ask, we ask in a not-so-sure sort of way that doesn't honour the God who's revealed himself not as the 'maybe' God but the 'immeasurably more than we could ask or imagine' God.[27]

If you don't ask to experience forgiveness and cleansing and the joy of salvation *big*, you'll miss out big, as some folks flying with Canadian airline WestJet found out, differently, a few years ago. It was Christmastime. At the departure gate before their flight, passengers were asked what they wanted from Santa Claus. What they didn't know was that WestJet had decided to grant all their requests. When they arrived at their destination, the luggage belt delivered lots of wrapped-up Christmas presents. Everyone got what they'd asked for, including the guy we feel sorry for, who only asked for socks when other people got expensive smartphones and an HDTV.[28]

In 1 John 1.9 God has turned a prayer he finds impossible to say no to into a promise. He doesn't even say 'ask for forgiveness'; he just says, 'if you confess I *will* forgive'. No maybes, no buts. If you humbly accept God's verdict about your sin, confess and mean it, he will forgive you, however bad you think you are and whatever wrongs you've done. He'll completely take away the guilt *and* the grime, the stain *and* the shame of sin. *And* he will give you joy. Joy in knowing him. Joy in knowing you don't have to live with a scarcity mindset any more because the most generous being in the universe is looking out for you. This knowing will liberate you to generous giving. Forgiving others freely who've hurt you. Being generous with your time, talents and treasures, because you want others to know this God and to honour his extraordinary generosity.

Questions for reflection

What should we learn from creation about God's generosity?

In what ways have you questioned God's generous disposition?

How does Jesus demonstrate God's glorious, uproarious, absurd generosity?

How generous do you think God is, therefore, with forgiveness?

How is God challenging you to be more generous?

Prayer of Confession
Holy Lord, I have sinned times without number, and been guilty of pride and unbelief, of failure to find thy mind in thy Word, of neglect to seek thee in my daily life. My transgressions and shortcomings present me with a list of accusations, but I bless thee that they will not stand against me, for all have been laid on Christ; go on to subdue my corruptions, and grant me grace to live above them.
  The Valley of Vision, a Collection of Puritan Prayers and Devotions, sixteenth to seventeenth centuries, compiled by Arthur Bennett

Forgiveness story #9

MICAH

I lost my virginity at fifteen. It was callous carelessness – a complete failure to understand the seriousness of sin despite growing up in a good Christian setting. I didn't consider the consequences; I just went with what seemed right to me at the time. But boy was it wrong. I went on to sleep with several other women. Some believe this is the secret to a happy life. I think they're foolish because it sucked all the goodness out of mine. I became emotionally numb, shut down inside, living a black-and-white existence without fully realising it. I continued to be active in church but unaware of how distant from God I'd become.

It took several years for conviction of sin to penetrate my hardened heart. I had just started at university. I was alone, separated from familiar friends and family. I'd slept with a girl the night before but this time it was different. I woke up feeling broken, horribly dirty. I cried. I realised for the first time how responsible I was for this sinful behaviour. I confessed that night's sin to God and had a fantastic experience of forgiveness. It wasn't a great prayer. I'm embarrassed how little I actually repented of – one night instead of four years of wayward living, offending God and dishonouring all those women. I see that now. But in his grace God still forgave me back then.

I started a sin–shame–forgiveness cycle. Things would go on like this for a while. I would fall into sexual sin, I would pray, and God would forgive me, again and again, but I couldn't break free. Around this time, I joined a good Christian group at university. They helped me understand how bad sin is, which helped me see more clearly the costly love of the cross. Things came together at a Bible festival a year or so later. A preacher spoke about people getting unstuck by the power of the Holy Spirit. I heard God speaking to me. I wanted to break free from this debilitating pattern of living. By this point, I'd confessed my sins to God in a much deeper way. I'd shared and become accountable to Godly mentors, but I hadn't told my earthly father. I was too fearful and ashamed, but that was exactly what I sensed God encouraging me to do that night, so I went for a walk with my dad. I broke down as I shared through many tears. After I'd unloaded, my earthly father gently laughed and said, 'Son, I never expected you to be perfect. I just want you to love Jesus.' At that moment I heard my Heavenly Father speaking powerfully. I was undone. My emotions were unlocked. I experienced the world in colour again. God's unmerited favour – grace – became more real to me than ever. I can't even say 'grace' without smiling or even laughing now. That night I experienced forgiveness on a level like nothing I'd known before. I've never slept around again. Sure, I've been tempted. Of course, I still sin in all sorts of ways, but I seek to confess my sins daily now. I don't want to allow myself to become distant again from the loving God of amazing grace. How could I, when he has been so good to me?

9

Cleanse us from all unrighteousness

'My faith is in the idea that God and His love are greater than whatever sins any of us commit.'

Rich Mullins

Have you ever been a victim of pigeon poo? I have. It's one of the horrible hazards of London living. You're minding your own business when suddenly, out of nowhere, boom, splatter. 'What was that?' you say to yourself as you instinctively, foolishly, reach up to touch the point of impact, only to smear your hand in excrement as poop starts to run down the side of your face. Superstitious people say it's a blessing but it's more like a curse. You feel dirty. Embarrassed. People start looking at you differently, turning their noses up, keeping their distance. I want to wash it off and begin my day again.

This is not dissimilar to what sin does to us – others' and our own. But the defilement isn't just on the outside; we're not just victims but also perpetrators. What if some wrong you've done or some important good you've failed to do is giving you a shame-saturated, not-good-enough identity? Maybe you're like me. When I sin, I want to withdraw into secrecy. I want to hide the part of me that transgressed. It's too humiliatingly dirty to be on display, so I only share the parts I consider socially acceptable.

This is a big problem in the Church because it means many suffer in silence. For example, women who've had abortions, which is one in three in their lifetime in the UK, and the men who encouraged them. They can be shamed into silence, afraid of what people might say or what God might do if they confess. Lots of people in church are hiding. Consider the shockingly high percentage of men and women with a porn habit, making themselves presentable on Sundays when beneath the surface they're battling almost unbearable shame. The equation, more or less, works like this: because I've *done* that, I *am* this. Because I've *done* wrong, I *am* wrong. Flawed. Useless. Worthless. You end up attacking yourself and/or attacking others. This is shame acting out. Sure, as we wrote in the Introduction, you can experience shame not from having sinned yourself but by being a victim of another's sin or as a result of living in a sin-soaked world full of suffering. But we inevitably react sinfully in response to being sinned against and other bad things happening to us, which brings on the guilt, feeling rotten, which activates the shame, feeling dirty.

It doesn't have to be that way. 'If we confess our sins,' God, through the blood of Jesus, *must* 'cleanse us from all unrighteousness'. The word 'cleanse' means wash away. Sins are purified from you. Every dirty trace of sin is removed. This is about being and feeling completely clean in the sight of God. Let's flesh this out by way of two historical case studies.

The leprous man

First, the leprous man from Matt. 8.1–4.[1] We suggest you read it now. Jesus has just preached his famous Sermon on the Mount, which began in chapter 5. He said, we paraphrase, unless your righteousness *exceeds* that of the super-religious 'do-gooding' Pharisees, you're toast. Jesus said flourishing[2] is about humbly hungering for righteousness. It isn't just about not committing murder but about not getting angry. Flourishing isn't only about not committing adultery, it's about not lusting full stop . . . and so on. Jesus called his followers to an incredibly high standard of moral purity. But it's so high for them, and for us today, it seems impossible, right? Perhaps that's his point. This, we believe, is confirmed by what Matthew reports as the first thing Jesus does the moment he finishes teaching.[3] He comes down from the mountainside and *cleanses* a man of leprosy. FYI, it's the same word in Greek as 1 John 1.9.

'Leprosy' today is a narrow term. Back then it was much broader, a catch-all concept for horrible, ugly, visible skin conditions. Metaphorically, it is an outward picture of what's inside the human heart. Lepers were the ultimate social outcasts, not allowed to have contact with people; many had to wear bells so you could hear them coming and flee. They're the people you don't want to sit next to or be seen with – they smell or have a criminal record – but more importantly they're the part of *you* that you don't want to be with.

Think of what happens to a person deprived of human contact. We go a bit crazy, like Tom Hanks in the film *Cast Away*. A volleyball becomes his best friend, unimaginatively called Wilson. Or consider Juan Mann, who was feeling so depressed and lonely he decided to begin the Free Hugs campaign. He once received a hug from a stranger that made him feel like a king, so he decided to stand on a street corner with a sign offering free hugs. You have a choice. You can start making your 'free hugs' sign or you can do what this leper did: get on your knees, admit your need and seek an embrace that's better than anything in this world.

The leprous man kneels before Jesus. That's a position of humility. It's as if he's saying, 'I know I'm a sinner. I know I'm unclean.' He doesn't ask to be healed. He asks to be made clean. Do you have the courage to do that? Then he says, 'if you are willing'.[4] He doesn't question Jesus' ability. He's sure Jesus is able; he must have heard stories about what Jesus was saying and doing. His question is more, 'Do you have enough compassion to help me? Am I too far gone? If you touch me, won't I make you unclean?' Isn't that what you are sometimes tempted to think?

'All.' Take a look at that word again in 1 John 1.9. It's rather inclusive, isn't it? Whatever you've done, however condemned you feel,

God is greater than your heart.[5] You are not too far gone. Jesus is willing.

What happens next is shocking. Twenty-first-century Westerners struggle to fully see just how shocking, so imagine the US president or the supreme leader of North Korea reaching to press the nuclear weapons launch button. We know that's probably not what happens, but please play along for a moment. As whoever's hand goes to touch it first, we would surely all be saying, 'NOOOOOOOOOOOOOOOO!' because it would be an act of extreme self-destruction: global thermal nuclear war and all that.

That's how we believe people in the crowd would have been thinking as Jesus reached to touch the leper. 'What are you doing, don't do it, you'll make yourself sick and unclean!' we imagine them saying, or rather screaming and shouting, to themselves. But to the shocked onlookers, Jesus' holy cleanness was more contagious than the man's uncleanness. 'Immediately'! 'Immediately' he was cleansed. What they saw happen externally, every trace of leprosy gone, happens internally the moment you confess your sins. You are cleansed of all unrighteousness.

The immoral woman

In the second case study, we meet the immoral woman from Sychar, Samaria, in John 4.1–42. We often tell this story as a 'be like Jesus' story. Listen compassionately as Jesus did. Do prophetic evangelism as Jesus did. But you won't be able to do any of that powerfully unless you have the humility to see yourself in this immoral woman (just as we trust you saw yourself in the leprous man).

She's getting water at noon, the start of the hottest hour of the day, when people ordinarily seek shade, eat a light meal or take a siesta. We think she's self-isolating because of shame.[6] She wouldn't be welcome to get water at the normal time with others from her town. She also probably doesn't want their judgemental pride or pity. She's had five husbands and is living immorally with a man to whom she is not married. She is experiencing the shame of being sinned against – perhaps some or all of these men divorced her unfairly – but it's also the shame of her own sin, we speculate, from trying to fill a lonely emptiness inside through intimacy with a man outside of marriage, or not trusting God to provide and sleeping with a man for economic security.[7]

Even though others are, Jesus isn't concerned about sitting with her. She's the reason they've gone through Samaria. Jesus doesn't go to the local religious leaders; he chooses to meet with this shame-filled woman. It is to her he reveals his true identity, the One who can quench the deepest longings for love. Jesus' presence transforms her as he helps her to stop hiding in the darkness and walk in the light. Or in other words, to confess. 'Go, call your husband,' he says.

'I have no husband,' she replies.

'Ahh,' Jesus, we imagine, says knowingly, smiling. 'You are right in saying, "I have no husband"; for you have had five husbands, and the one you now have is not your husband. What you have said is true' (John 4.17b–18). It is as if a fleshing out of the final verses of Ps. 139 is taking place: 'Search me, O God . . . See if there is any griev-ous way in me, and lead me in the way everlasting.' Jesus is expos-ing her uncleanness, but not in a condemning way. Can you see that? He's gently helping her to own her sin, which she implicitly does by responding, 'I perceive that you are a prophet' (John 4.19). 'You are right about me,' she is saying. Jesus is leading her into everlasting life.

What happens next in the story is profoundly moving. This woman runs to the very people she has been hiding from to tell them about Jesus. What a transformation! We imagine her jumping with joy, unable to get the words out fast enough – she is just so ex-cited. She testifies: 'He told me all that I ever did' (John 4.39b). This is strange because according to the biblical account, he hasn't. Jesus has sensitively told her only about her relationships. But it's as if sin has so defined her it has become her identity. Has yours?

Her faith in Jesus has made her new. Her sin is no longer a cause for shame but celebration. She is clean! Her past doesn't define her anymore. Its stain is gone. And her transformation touches an entire town, as many come to believe that Jesus is the Saviour of the world. The way into the centre is often through people on the edge.

But wait, there is more. Wells throughout Scripture are meeting places that lead to marriage.[8] John specifically reminds us of this by pointing out that this is happening at what became of Jacob's well, connecting us back to Gen. 29, where Jacob met and married Rachel. The Samaritan woman can be seen to represent Jewish and Gentile unfaithfulness, going as far back as the disobedient ten northern tribes of Israel and their subsequent intermixing with pagan non-Jews, originally Assyrians.[9] Having just been referred to as the 'bridegroom' (John 3.29) in the preceding chapter, Jesus is coming as the perfect *seventh* husband. He's like a true and better Hosea reaching out to the unfaithful wife Gomer, figuratively the people of God, alluring her and speaking 'tenderly to her' (Hos. 2.14), turning our valley of sinful trouble into a doorway of confessional hope. It is a picture of Jesus wooing the bride of Christ, his Jewish–Gentile Church.

The washed worshipper

Jesus became the ultimate leper. He died the most shameful death imaginable so he could sit beside you. He's waiting for you to kneel inside. He's waiting to hear your confession. He's waiting to set you free. He's waiting for you to run and tell the world what he's done. God is so willing he came from heaven to earth to die for you. He disregarded the shame of the cross for you[10] so you can purchase, at his extraordinary expense, 'white garments so that you may clothe yourself and the shame of your nakedness may not be seen' (Rev. 3.18). Or in other words, though your sins are red like scarlet, he washes them white as snow.[11] He sprinkles you clean with his blood and puts his Spirit in you.[12] He washes you thoroughly from iniquity and creates a clean heart inside you.[13]

In short, God wants renewed *fellowship* with you.

He wants you to know joy unspeakable and full of glory – 'to the praise of his glorious *grace*' (Eph. 1.6a).[14] Knowing this will empower you to say no to sin and to flourish, because you're not operating on human willpower now but heavenly love power, through faith in Christ.

So, when you sin and get infected with leprosy again, and you will, know that Jesus 'comes down' *immediately* to clean you up the moment you confess – because he is faithful. And just. To forgive us our sins. And. Cleanse us from all unrighteousness. In the words of inspirational ragamuffin worship leader Rich Mullins:

I think I would rather live on the verge of falling and let my security be in the all-sufficiency of the grace of God than to live in some pietistic illusion of moral excellence. Not that I don't want to be morally excellent but my faith isn't in the idea that I'm more moral than anybody else. My faith is in the idea that God and His love are greater than whatever sins any of us commit.[15]

Questions for reflection

How have your sins made you feel ashamed?

In what ways can you identify with the leprous man and the immoral woman?

How can their encounters with Jesus encourage you to confess your sins?

Prayer of Confession
Merciful Father, I feel worn down and heavy.
I'm sorry for the hypocrite I can be.
I'm sorry for hiding my darkness from you. I avoid you, even though I know opening up to you is what's best for me.
I'm sorry for tailoring a false image of myself to other people rather than embracing your process of transformation.
Forgive me for how judgemental my heart can be to others.
Forgive me for the anger I can feel in my mind towards them.
Forgive me for believing my identity is in my own hands rather than created and shaped by you.
Thank you for speaking forgiveness and grace over all my sins.
Thank you for never giving up on me.
Thank you for loving me with a steadfast love.
Amen.

Holly Satterthwaite, twenty-first century

10
Application

'Have mercy on me, O God, according to your steadfast love.'

Ps. 51.1

I (Holly) have a friend who recently shared how much her husband loves antiques. He scours markets and shops for the best finds. He watches TV programmes on antiques most nights and loves to follow bidding wars. She said he even works with two computer screens open, one for his work and one for online antique auctions. So naturally I asked her, 'What has been his best buy?' 'Oh,' she said, 'he's never bought anything. It just always feels too risky to throw his hat in the ring.' I politely smiled, but inside I found myself asking, 'So what is it all for, then? Isn't he missing out on a greater measure of joy in his beloved hobby?' Confession can be a bit like that. We can read about it in our Bibles, in this book, and talk about the wonderful gift of forgiveness with others, but are we really making time to be alone with our Heavenly Father to practise this discipline and experience joyful liberation? Are we willing to step out and to go deeper into fellowship with God? How do we, practically, make this a habit?

When it comes to fellowship with God, we need to throw our figurative hats into the ring and not watch from the sidelines. This hat-throwing phrase originated in boxing. If someone wanted to fight, they could throw their hat into the boxing ring, and this let the referee know they wanted to challenge another person. We want to wage war on sin and the unholy trinity of the world, the flesh and the devil in the spiritual boxing ring with confession, shedding our guilt and shame with every punch. But let's be honest: sometimes the thought of that fight can make us feel exhausted before we even utter a word to God. We don't know where to start or how best to plead for mercy. Sometimes those feelings can prevent or at least delay us saying anything at all. But what we must remember is that Jesus has already won the victory on our behalf. As long as we're willing to step into the ring, we can fail to fully land any punches and still be crowned winners by his grace.

This chapter outlines some tools and guides to get you started and encourage you on the way, to help you cultivate the discipline of confession.

Written confessions

Each chapter of this book concluded with a written confession from the Bible or the pen of an early Church leader. We hope you've enjoyed using them and will continue to do so, to help you form your own meaning-rich words that bring the joy of confession personally alive to you. We have intentionally collated these for you to use in your confession times with God – to read them aloud, meditate on them in your heart and/or rewrite them in your own words. They provide a helpful structure for confessing your sin.

Scriptural confessions

Sometimes there can be days when confession, like any prayer, can feel rather dutiful. We'll be honest that sometimes, especially when we're busy or tired, we can approach it like a box-ticking exercise rather than with the spirit of a panting deer drawing close to the source of living water. On these days, praying Scripture can be especially helpful because the Bible isn't just words on the page. Heb. 4.12 tells us, 'the word of God is living and active, sharper than any two-edged sword, piercing to the division of soul and of spirit, of joints and of marrow, and discerning the thoughts and intentions of the heart'. Scripture is alive through the Holy Spirit, and as you read and recite it, the Holy Spirit is at work, using it to bring conviction, highlight sin and align your heart with heaven. God ministers to you as you speak his words back to him.

Let's use Ps. 51 as an example. By way of reminder, David wrote this powerful confession after sexual sin and murder.[1] The grief at his sin is obvious, as are his love and reverence for God. We see his 'man after God's own heart'[2] disposition revealed in vulnerable, emotionally raw repentance. Read the psalm slowly, reflect on the questions below and then pray it aloud to God in these words and then your own.

Have mercy on me, O God,
    according to your steadfast love;
according to your abundant mercy
    blot out my transgressions.
Wash me thoroughly from my iniquity,
    and cleanse me from my sin!

For I know my transgressions,
    and my sin is ever before me.
Against you, you only, have I sinned
    and done what is evil in your sight,
so that you may be justified in your words
    and blameless in your judgement.
Behold, I was brought forth in iniquity,
    and in sin did my mother conceive me.
Behold, you delight in truth in the inward being,
    and you teach me wisdom in the secret heart.

Purge me with hyssop, and I shall be clean;
    wash me, and I shall be whiter than snow.
Let me hear joy and gladness;
    let the bones that you have broken rejoice.
Hide your face from my sins,
    and blot out all my iniquities.

Create in me a clean heart, O God,
  and renew a right spirit within me.
Cast me not away from your presence,
  and take not your Holy Spirit from me.
Restore to me the joy of your salvation,
  and uphold me with a willing spirit.

Then I will teach transgressors your ways,
  and sinners will return to you.
Deliver me from bloodguiltiness, O God,
  O God of my salvation,
  and my tongue will sing aloud of your righteousness.
O Lord, open my lips,
  and my mouth will declare your praise.
For you will not delight in sacrifice, or I would give it;
  you will not be pleased with a burnt offering.
The sacrifices of God are a broken spirit;
  a broken and contrite heart, O God, you will not despise.

Do good to Zion in your good pleasure;
  build up the walls of Jerusalem;
then will you delight in right sacrifices,
  in burnt offerings and whole burnt offerings;
  then bulls will be offered on your altar.

What is the sin that is before you today? Do you feel the weight of it? Notice David's descriptions of broken bones, feeling unclean, anxiety at being cast out of God's presence, cut off from the Holy Spirit, and needing restoration of joy. Knowing your salvation is secure and God will uphold you with a willing spirit, how will your mouth declare his praise? How does it feel to know that God will not despise a broken and contrite heart but delights in your coming to him?

Historical confessions

Here we engage with liturgy. Some love it; others hate it. 'Boring,' they say. But liturgy can help you engage with God, especially when you're physically or emotionally exhausted, worn out and unable to think what to say. Liturgy literally means 'work for the people'. It is the public service of great saints of old for you. They have so much to teach us. As Deut. 32.7 puts it, 'Remember the days of old; consider the years of many generations; ask your father, and he will show you, your elders, and they will tell you.' Society, knowledge and technology may have raced ahead of them, but we have not progressed beyond their wisdom. We would argue that their contribution to our spiritual formation is even more precious because of its separation from the influence of modern technology and the current cultural norms that shape us so instinctively.

Reading these confessions is a rich reminder of God's faithfulness to generation after generation of his people. His character, love and offer of fellowship are consistent across all times, cultures and nations. It reminds us that when we struggle, we're not alone, and that our wrestling is nothing new. You can't shock God with your sin; he's been dealing with this dirt and grime for centuries. He's been gracious and merciful for millennia. Reading our forebears' honest prayers not only draws us closer into fellowship with God but also highlights the fellowship we share with the global Church. Billions of people, all with their own logs that need removing from their eyes.[3] We do not journey with God in isolation; we have a shared experience of failure, forgiveness and joy. One day we will not know the deceased authors of these confessions merely as names of dead people on a page but as living people whom we will spend eternity with, sharing our stories of God's mercy and grace.

One of our favourite historical prayers of confession comes from *The Valley of Vision*, a collection of Puritan prayers and devotionals. Try reading it several times and reflecting on the questions below.

O GOD OF GRACE,
Thou hast imputed my sin to my substitute,
    and hast imputed his righteousness
    to my soul,
    clothing me with a bridegroom's robe,
    decking me with jewels of holiness.
But in my Christian walk I am still in rags;
    my best prayers are stained with sin;
    my penitential tears are so much impurity;
    my confessions of wrong are so many
        aggravations of sin;
    my receiving the Spirit is tinctured with
        selfishness.
I need to repent of my repentance;
I need my tears to be washed;
I have no robe to bring to cover my sins,
    no loom to weave my own righteousness;
I am always standing clothed in filthy garments,
    and by grace am always receiving change of
        raiment,
    for thou dost always justify the ungodly;
I am always going into the far country,
    and always returning home as a prodigal,
    always saying, Father, forgive me,
    and thou art always bringing forth
        the best robe.
Every morning let me wear it,
    every evening return in it,
    go out to the day's work in it,
    be married in it,
    be wound in death in it,
    stand before the great white throne in it,
    enter heaven in it shining as the sun.

Grant me never to lose sight of
   the exceeding sinfulness of sin,
   the exceeding righteousness of salvation,
   the exceeding glory of Christ,
   the exceeding beauty of holiness,
   the exceeding wonder of grace.

How is God not just *a* or even *the* 'God of grace' but the '*O* God', the awesome, amazing God of grace? How do you experience his unmerited favour? Why is it important to start your prayer with such a glorious declaration? Take a moment to lament over the struggle to resist sin. What particular sins are 'always' taking you 'into the far country'? Give thanks to God for him 'always bringing forth the best robe'. What does it feel like to wear this privileged, fully forgiven status? Ask God to open your eyes to more clearly see the fullness of the gospel and the 'exceeding wonder of grace'. Note that the prayer is bookended by grace.

Look back through all the prayers of confession in this book and similarly meditate on them.

Practical acts

The Old Testament has several examples of people building physical altars to God to remember his faithfulness. Think of Jacob turning his rock pillow into a pillar of stones serving as an altar at Bethel,[4] and Joshua's twelve stones to preserve the memory of the miraculous crossing of the river Jordan.[5] Now we're not suggesting you start to pile up rocks in your bedroom, but there is something helpful about having a practical reminder of confession and the freedom it brings, to help us keep our eyes on Jesus through the ordinariness of life. It could be a physical object, a one-off act or a regular practice. For example, I have a framed picture hanging in my office of a collection of objects related to my pre-Christian life with the words written above:

'You are no longer who you were.' When shame and guilt begin to eat away at me, I can glance up at my wall and remember I am cleansed and covered by the blood of Jesus. Perhaps you have something significant you might want to frame for your wall. Here are a few other suggestions:

Stones

Write your sins on a stone with chalk as you confess to God and then wash the stone, removing all trace of the writing, as you receive his forgiveness. Consider writing a personalised Scripture on it, perhaps modifying Isa. 1.18: 'Though my sins were red like scarlet, through Christ, they are white as snow.' Every time you feel guilt grow, look at or pick up that stone and remember the faithfulness of God who cleanses you from all unrighteousness.

Throwing it away

Sometimes, to help our hearts engage with the truth of our freedom, we have written the troubling sin down on paper and then scrunched it up and binned it – a physical act of the sin being take away and removed.

Journaling

We write down our prayers and confessions a lot. It is hugely encouraging to look back on things we journaled years ago and see how God has changed us both. By looking back at the struggles we used to have, we become more aware of the freedom we now walk in, and it gives us hope that God will help us through our current battles with sin. It also helps us keep the habit, as every time we pick up the pen and notebook it's a prompt to remember to confess. When you write your prayers, it becomes very obvious very quickly if your prayer life begins to consistently look like a Christmas gift list! It's important, though, that these journals serve as encouragement, not a record of your (or others'!) wrongs. We're not meant to dwell in condemnation but through confession to embrace more freedom and joy. To ensure this, it helps to ground confessional prayers in a good structure, like ACTS – adoration, confession, thanksgiving and supplication – or to bookend your journaled prayers with the grace of God, like in the example above. If you still find this becomes a source of self-attack for you, then we'd suggest focusing on other methods, at least initially.

Accountability

We have argued that confession of sin is first and foremost to God. But as John Calvin notes: 'A willing confession among men follows that secret confession which is made to God, as often as either divine glory or our humiliation demands it.'[6] Our humiliation often demands it, even if only to demonstrate that the shame is gone; it makes something personal and private more tangible and real. As some have testified in this book, sharing your confession of sin with someone else can cement your experience of forgiveness. When we seek to hide from others something we're struggling with deeply, we can't truly be ourselves around them. It leads to superficial and inauthentic fellowship with other believers. They can't strengthen and encourage you in the ways you need. They can't lovingly keep you accountable as you seek to walk out of a particular sin pattern. John Piper says, 'The principle is that dishonesty and hiddenness and privateness about our sins brings both spiritual and physical misery. God would spare us that, and so he teaches us to confess our sins to God and to one another.'[7] This doesn't, of course, mean telling everyone in your church about an ongoing porn or gossip addiction – that wouldn't help you or them. It does mean seeking out a select few you can trust, who have the maturity and love to come alongside you in the battle.

Sacraments

In his excellent book *Truth We Can Touch*, Tim Chester writes: 'The forgiveness of sin is not just something I feel. It is an objective reality that took place at the cross. And we have that promise in water, bread, and wine . . . God in his kindness, knowing how frail we are, knowing how battered by life we can be, also gives us physical reminders of his grace in water, bread, and wine.'[8] One-time-only water baptism and regular corporate celebration of what is variously called the Lord's Supper, Communion or Eucharist are sensory experiences, given by God to help you *objectively* taste and intimately know the loving sacrifice of Christ on the cross, to assure you of your total forgiveness and complete cleansing. Have you been baptised? Are you taking Communion regularly with your church?

Final encouragement

Just do it. Confession doesn't have to be perfect. Ours certainly isn't. It just needs to be real, authentic and honest. God is inviting you to experience the inexpressible joy of deeper fellowship with him. Don't miss out. Redeem confession to rejoice more richly in God. Slow down through confession to savour more sweetly the grace of God. Renew your soul with confession to open the door to revival – for the glory of God alone.

Notes

Introduction

1 Welch, E.T., *Shame Interrupted* (New Growth Press, 2012), p.2.

2 Frost, R., 'Desert Places' (*The Complete Poems of Robert Frost*, Jonathan Cape 1951): 'They cannot scare me with their empty spaces / Between stars – on stars where no human race is. / I have it in me so much nearer home / To scare myself with my own desert places.'

3 Like Adam and Eve in Eden, Gen. 3.8.

4 Waterlow, L., '"People Call Me an Oompa Loompa": Fake Tan Addict, 21, Who's Spent £30,000 on Bronzing Products Applies So Much Each Day That She Needs BLEACH to Remove It' (*Mail Online*, 1 June 2016), https://www.dailymail.co.uk/femail /article-3619780/Fake-tan-addict-spends-30-000-bronzing -products.html. For those who haven't read or seen Roald Dahl's *Charlie and the Chocolate Factory,* Oompa Loompas are orange- skinned fictional dwarves who make sweets and sarcastically give songs of advice.

5 To *Matrix* film fans, take the red pill.

6 Willard, D., *Renovation of the Heart: Putting on the Character of Christ* (IVP, 2002), p.174.

7 McClay, W.M., 'The Strange Persistence of Guilt' (*The Hedgehog Review*, spring 2017), https://hedgehogreview.com/issues /the-post-modern-self/articles/the-strange-persistence-of-guilt.

8 King, M.L., 'Rediscovering Lost Values' (*A Knock at Midnight: Inspiration From the Great Sermons of Reverend Martin Luther King, Jr.*, Carson, C., Holloran, P., eds., New York, Warner Books, 2000).

9 Pow, H., '"I Lost My Soul as Much as a Person Can and Still Be Walking Around": The Real Wolf of Wall Street Describes the First Time Greed Got the Better of Him as He Says He's Willing to Meet Victims of His Multimillion Dollar Fraud' (*Mail Online*, 21 January 2014), https://www.dailymail.co.uk/news /article-2543119/I-lost-soul-person-walking-The-real-Wolf-Wall -Street-describes-time-greed-got-better-says-hes-willing-meet -victims-multimillion-dollar-fraud.html. Italics added.

10 This is a reference to the brilliant convert from atheism and author of *The Chronicles of Narnia*, Professor C.S. Lewis. In *Mere Christianity* (Geoffrey Bles, 1952), he wrote: 'Human beings, all over the earth, have this curious idea that they ought to behave in a certain way, and cannot really get rid of it. Secondly, that they do not in fact behave that way. They know the Law of Nature; they break it. These facts are the foundation of all clear thinking about ourselves and the universe we live in.'

11 Ruse, M., 'Evolutionary Theory and Christian Ethics' (*The Darwinian Paradigm: Essays on Its History, Philosophy and Religious Implications*, Routledge, 1989), pp.262–9.

12 For more, see David Robertson's letter to Richard Dawkins titled 'The Myth of Godless Morality' in his book *The Dawkins Letters: Challenging Atheist Myths* (Christian Focus Publications, 2007).

13 Koberle, A., 'The Problem of Guilt' (*Pastoral Psychology*, 1957), pp.33–9, https://doi.org/10.1007/BF01785302.

14 Fame and fortune are no answer to guilt; they might even make it worse.

15 Moore, S., 'We Are in the Midst of a Mental Health Crisis – Advice About Jogging and Self-Care Is Not Enough' (*The Guardian*, 7 October 2019), https://www.theguardian.com /commentisfree/2019/oct/07/we-are-in-the-midst-of-a-mental -health-crisis-advice-about-jogging-and-self-care-is-not-enough.

16 Stott, J., *Confess Your Sins: The Way of Reconciliation* (Hodder & Stoughton, 1964), p.69.

17 Shakespeare, W., *Macbeth*, act 3, scene 2.

18 His name is Stephen Sloan and he deserves much praise. He and his wife, Gillian, have served faithfully and fruitfully for over forty years at Westminster Chapel. Thank you!

19 Not to mention all the other amazing preachers who've occupied the chapel's pulpit, from Mr 'Love-Your-Neighbour', Rev. Samuel Martin, the founding pastor who took the church from just twenty people to over 1,000 in twenty years, to the outstanding preacher and author of more than fifty top-selling books, Mr 'Word-and-Spirit', Dr R.T. Kendall.

20 Stott, *Confess Your Sins*. Excellent as it is, it's only partly about confession to God alone.

21 Lloyd-Jones, D.M., *Spiritual Depression: Its Causes and Cures* (Pickering and Inglis, 1965), pp.23, 28.

22 Reformer John Calvin said confession is like laying bare your wounds to the physician. Calvin, J., and Battles, F.L., *Calvin: Institutes of the Christian Religion* (Louisville, KY, Westminster John Knox Press, 2001), p.634.

23 Ortberg, J., *1 John: Love Each Other* (Grand Rapids, MI, Willow Creek Association, 1999), p.22.

24 The final purpose statement of the letter, 5.13, makes it clear he's writing to those who already believe in Jesus as the Son of God. John is writing to those whose 'sins *are* forgiven' (1 John 2.12, italics added), that they might 'see what kind of love the Father has given' them (1 John 3.1) through a deepening experience of forgiveness.

25 Ps. 32.3–4.

26 Ps. 51.8, 12, italics added.

27 Luke 15.11–32.

28 '*Shawshank Redemption*: Andy Escapes', https://www.youtube .com/watch?v=neO5fnwQjqg.

29 We've sourced stories from our church community, not, we trust, in a proud way, although we do love our local church family, but

because they are the testimonies we know, and to which we have access. Some people have used false names, indicated by a star (*), where we, with them, have felt it wise and/or necessary.

30 Allen, M., 'Sean Parker Unloads on Facebook: "God Only Knows What It's Doing to Our Children's Brains"' (Axios, 9 November 2017), https://www.axios.com/sean-parker-unloads -on-facebook-god-only-knows-what-its-doing-to-our-childrens -brains-1513306792-f855e7b4-4e99-4d60-8d51-2775559c2671 .html.

31 Atamaniuk, M., 'How Many Ads Do You Actually See Daily?!' (Clario, 21 April 2020), https://stopad.io/blog/ads-seen-daily.

32 Lovelace, R., *Dynamics of Spiritual Life: An Evangelical Theology of Renewal* (IVP, 1979), p.13.

33 Patterson, N. *Change of the Tide: Revivals in the UK* (Regeneration Publications, 2020), p.152.

I If

1 Microsoft 'To Do' advert, https://www.youtube.com /watch?v=6k3_T84z5Ds.

2 Inspired by a joke by the British comedian Michael McIntyre.

3 Barr, S., 'What Is Quitter's Day and When Does It Take Place?' (*The Independent*, 17 January 2020), https://www.independent.co.uk /life-style/quitters-day-new-years-resolutions-fitness-january -exercise-active-strava-a9288556.html.

4 Lloyd-Jones, D.M., *Life in Christ: Studies in 1 John* (Wheaton, IL, Crossway Books, 2002), p.728.

5 2 Kings 11.1.

6 Matt. 5–7.

7 If you want to know more about Howard's story, watch this video: https://vimeo.com/132521964

8 At least in our opinion – please don't sue us.

9 The wonderful David Shearman, former senior pastor of the Christian Centre, Nottingham, now Heart Church.

10 NIV translation.

11 Maxwell, J.C., *Talent Is Never Enough: Discover the Choices That Will Take You Beyond Your Talent* (Thomas Nelson, 2007), p.10.

12 Luke 10.25–37.

13 Tacitus (AD 56–120), Roman historian: 'Christians derived their name from a man called Christ, who during the reign of Emperor Tiberius had been executed by sentence of the procurator Pontius Pilate . . .'; Lucian (AD 115–200), Greek satirist, refers to the founder of Christianity this way: 'the one whom they still worship today, the man in Palestine who was crucified because he brought this new form of initiation into the world . . .'; Josephus (AD 37–100), Jewish historian – this is (non-Christian) Professor Geza Vermes' reconstruction: 'About this time there lived Jesus, a wise man . . . For he was one who performed paradoxical deeds and was the teacher of such people as accept the truth gladly. He won over many Jews [and many Greeks?]. He was [called] the Christ. When Pilate, upon hearing him accused by men of the highest standing among us, had condemned him to be crucified, those who had in the first place come to love him did not give up their affection for him . . . And the tribe of the Christians, so called after him, has still to this day not disappeared.' Vermas, G., 'Jesus in the Eyes of Josephus' (*Standpoint.*, 14 December 2019), https://standpointmag.co.uk/jesus-in-the-eyes-of-josephus-features-jan-10-geza-vermes.

14 If you're wondering whether you can trust that their testimony has been recorded and translated accurately down through the centuries, read Peter J. Williams' superb book, *Can We Trust the Gospels?* (Wheaton, IL, Crossway, 2018).

15 This is one of the many myths our culture teaches that aren't true. There's even a behaviour named after Napoleon based on compensating for shortness, the Napoleon complex. Only he wasn't short. He was 5'2" in French units, the equivalent of 5'6½" in modern measurement units. He was average height for his time.

How many (propaganda-like) myths do people today believe about Christianity that aren't true?

16 'Are These Remarks by Napoleon on Jesus Genuine?' (History Stack Exchange), https://history.stackexchange.com/questions/7560 /are-these-remarks-by-napoleon-on-jesus-genuine. See comments 7 and 8.

17 If you can spare 114 seconds, watch the ending here: https://www .youtube.com/watch?v=zRBl0GPBm4o.

2 We

1 We're deliberately not citing this one because we don't want it to make this a personal attack against an individual; this thinking is shared by many and would be by us, but for the grace of God.

2 We mean that – it's one of the many sins we need to detox from.

3 Niles, D.T., *That They May Have Life* (New York, Harper, in association with the Student Volunteer Movement for Christian Missions, 1951), p.96.

4 Osborne, S., 'American Man Refuses to Find Out Who Won the US Presidential Election After Donald Trump's Victory' (*The Independent*, 20 November 2016), https://www.independent.co.uk /news/world/americas/donald-trump-us-presidential-election -man-refuses-to-find-out-who-won-a7428136.html.

5 Dr Michael Eaton tells the story at 35:35 here: https://www .westminsterchapel.org.uk/sermons/finding-fellowship-with -god-part-3.

6 Along with Matt Chandler of the Village Church, Texas, USA, who originally gave us this idea in one of his many super sermons.

7 Lewis, C.S., *Mere Christianity* (Harper Collins, 1997), p.100.

8 John 6.67–8: '"You do not want to leave too, do you?" Jesus asked the Twelve. Simon Peter answered him, "Lord, to whom shall we go? You have the words of eternal life. We have come to believe and to know that you are the Holy One of God."'

9 Edwords, F., 'What Is Humanism?' (American Humanist Association), https://americanhumanist.org/what-is-humanism/edwords-what-is-humanism.

10 Brahm, A., 'On Guilt' (Buddhist Society of Western Australia, 6 November 2015), https://bswa.org/teaching/guilt-by-ajahn-brahm-2.

11 Assuming, of course, you weren't really bad in the past life, because that would mean being reincarnated as a wild beast or something.

12 Qur'an: suras 7.6–9; 35.7. Even Muhammad himself was unsure of his salvation (see suras 31.34; 46.9).

13 Jer. 25.25; Isa. 51.17; Matt. 20.20–8; 26.39.

3 Confess

1 A confession – or is it? Keep reading to make an informed decision.

2 Bonhoeffer, D., *Life Together and Prayerbook of the Bible* (Minneapolis, MN, Fortress Press, 2015), p.90. Although Bonhoeffer makes this statement primarily about confession to others in the community of faith, the principle holds true for all forms of confession.

3 Manton, T., *A Practical Exposition of James* (Samuel Holdsworth, Paternoster, 1840), p.206.

4 Gryboski, M., 'Union Seminary Mocked for Having Students Confess to Plants' (*Christian Post*, 20 September 2019), https://www.christianpost.com/news/union-seminary-mocked-for-having-students-confess-to-plants.html.

5 Heb. 4.16.

6 Lloyd-Jones, D.M., *Life in Christ: Studies in 1 John* (Wheaton, IL, Crossway, 2002), p.123.

7 Shaggy, 'It Wasn't Me.' 2000.

8 Fawbert, D., 'How to Apologise Without Actually Apologising' (*ShortList*, 15 November 2017), https://www.shortlist.com/news/how-to-apologise-without-apologising-non-apology.

9 2 Corinthians 7.10.

10 Heb. 12.16–17.

11 1 Sam. 15.

12 1 Sam. 15.12b.

13 Joel 2.13.

14 Ps. 51.4.

15 NIV translation.

16 1 John 1.7.

17 One drachma is said by classical historians to be equivalent to a day's wages for a skilled worker. This is very rough working, but using the average UK person's annual salary of £30,000, one drachma equates to £82.19; multiply by 50,000 (drachmas) and you get £4.1 million.

18 1 John 5.13.

19 1 John 1.4.

20 John 16.8.

21 Ps. 139.23–4.

22 Luke 2.41–52.

23 The meaning of the word 'grieve' in Greek here is to 'make sad', so at least from a human point of view it is possible to hurt God's feelings, despite God's emotions from a higher vantage point being unchanging. God is impassible, to use the theological term, but he has condescended to our level through his great plan of salvation, mysteriously making it possible for us to hurt him in some way.

24 Only persons, not forces, can be grieved.

25 John 1.32.

26 Rom. 8.15–17.

27 Acts 1.8.

28 Inspired by Martin Lloyd-Jones' sermon 'Grieve Not the Holy Spirit of God' in *Darkness and Delight: An Exposition of Ephesians 4:17 to 5:17* (Banner of Truth, 1982), p.275. Lloyd-Jones affirms, 'when I say the Spirit withdraws Himself, I do not mean He goes

out of you; He still says there, but the gracious manifestations are withdrawn.'

29 Italics added.

30 Isa. 6.2.

31 John 13:10 quote, this is from NIV 1984.

32 Phil. 4.8.

4 Our sins

1 Saner, E., 'Why Do So Many Men Think They Could Win a Point Off Serena Williams?' (*The Guardian*, 15 July 2019), https://www.theguardian.com/sport/shortcuts/2019/jul/15/why-do-so-many-men-think-they-could-win-a-point-off-serena-williams.

2 'Would Serena Williams Lose a Point to an Average Man? She Gives Emphatic Answer in Hilarious Demo' (*Tennishead*, 22 July 2019), https://tennishead.net/would-serena-williams-lose-a-point-to-an-average-man-she-gives-emphatic-answer-in-hilarious-demo.

3 Lovelace, *Dynamics of Spiritual Life* (expanded edn), p.18.

4 Rom. 12.1–2.

5 Adopting, for example, the Western world's attitude to abortion, calling the killing of 40–50 million unborn children a year (not to save the life of the mother, but mostly for the personal convenience of the parents) morally good; see Jones, S., 'Abortion Is Morally Good' (*Intelligencer*, 17 May 2019), https://nymag.com/intelligencer/2019/05/theres-nothing-wrong-with-abortion.html. Has the Church been squeezed by the world to remain silent rather than to speak up with grace and truth for these children, who cannot speak for themselves?

6 Sloat, S., 'Science Explains How "Never Gonna Give You Up" Lived for 30 Years' (*Inverse*, 28 July 2017), https://www.inverse.com/article/34801-never-gonna-give-you-up-rick-astley-earworm-science.

7 Calvin and Battles, *Calvin*, p.602.

8 Owen, J., *Overcoming Sin and Temptation* (Kapic, K., Taylor, J., eds., Wheaton, IL, Crossway, 2015), p.27.

9 *Ibid.*, p.50.

10 Delbanco, A., *The Death of Satan: How Americans Have Lost the Sense of Evil* (New York, Farrar, Straus and Giroux, 1995), p.9.

11 John 8.44.

12 John 10.10.

13 2 Cor. 11.14.

14 1 Pet. 5.8.

15 Rev. 12.9–10.

16 Gen. 3.7–10.

17 Col. 2.15.

18 Eph. 6.12.

19 Gen. 4.4.

20 Lennox, J., 'If God, Why Coronavirus?' (*Premier Christianity*, 7 April 2020), https://www.premierchristianity.com/Blog /John-Lennox-If-God-why-coronavirus.

21 Wilberforce, W., *A Practical View of Christianity* (Massachusetts, Hendrickson Publishers, 1996), p.158. We are thankful to John Piper who led us to read this quote, and the one that follows it, in context.

22 *Ibid.*, p.160.

23 Rom. 1.18–23 comes before the behaviours listed in verses 24–32, e.g., 'shameful lusts'.

24 Piper, J., 'Sin Prefers Anything to God' (desiringGod.org, 8 April 2015), https://www.desiringgod.org/interviews/sin -prefers-anything-to-god.

25 1 John 3.12.

26 Matt. 5–7.

27 Kassian, M.A., *The Right Kind of Strong* (Nashville, TN, Nelson Books, 2019), pp.85–6.

28 We benefitted greatly from the way Kevin deYoung so ably explained this in his blog: DeYoung, K., 'Temptation Is Not

the Same as Sin' (The Gospel Coalition, 26 September 2013), https://www.thegospelcoalition.org/blogs/kevin-deyoung /temptation-is-not-the-same-as-sin.

29 Breen, M., *Multiplying Missional Leaders* (Greenville, SC, 3DM, 2012), pp.19–46.

30 Weinman, S., 'Why We Still Look Away: Kitty Genovese, Jamie Bulger and the Bystander Effect' (*The Guardian*, 9 April 2016), https://www.theguardian.com/society/2016/apr/09 /kitty-genovese-jamie-bulger-bystander-effect.

31 Gal. 6.1.

32 Henry, J., 'Words Associated With Christianity and British History Taken Out of Children's Dictionary' (*Telegraph*, 6 December 2008), https://www.telegraph.co.uk/education/3569045/Words -associated-with-Christianity-and-British-history-taken-out-of -childrens-dictionary.html.

33 Lloyd-Jones, *Spiritual Depression* (1979 reprint), pp.67–8.

34 1 Tim. 1.13–14.

35 Rom. 5.20.

36 But, you might be thinking, you've committed the unforgiveable sin (Mark 3.28–30; Matt. 12.31–2). This sin is deliberately resisting the Holy Spirit's witness and invitation to turn to Jesus. It is persistent, wilful refusal to repent, to bow to Jesus, even with your dying breath. If you're worried that you have committed it, that's almost certainly proof that you haven't.

37 John 6.37.

5 He is faithful

1 Matt. 26.33–5.

2 Alpert, D., 'On the Origin of Everything' (*New York Times*, 23 March 2012), https://www.nytimes.com/2012/03/25/books/review /a-universe-from-nothing-by-lawrence-m-krauss.html.

3 NIV translation.

4 Prov. 6.6.

5 Jer. 31.35–6; 33.20.

6 Psalm 130:6.

7 We are indebted to Tim Mackie of the brilliant BibleProject fame for his insights on this passage.

8 Merritt, D., 'Voltaire's Prediction, Home, and the Bible Society: Truth or Myth?' (*Bellator Christi*, 18 March 2019), https://bellatorchristi.com/2019/03/18/voltaires-prediction-home-and-the-bible-society-truth-or-myth.

9 Hackett, C., and McClendon, D., 'Christians Remain the World's Largest Religious Group, but They Are Declining in Europe' (Pew Research Center, 5 April 2017), https://www.pewresearch.org/fact-tank/2017/04/05/christians-remain-worlds-largest-religious-group-but-they-are-declining-in-europe.

10 Wilkin, J., *In His Image: 10 Ways God Calls Us to Reflect His Character* (Wheaton, IL, Crossway, 2018), p.97.

6 And just

1 Lewis, *Mere Christianity* (1997 edn), p.7.

2 Miller, A., *After the Fall* (*The Penguin Arthur Miller: Collected Plays, 1915 – The Miller Centennial – 2015*, Penguin, 2015), p.3.

3 Dawkins, R., *River Out of Eden: A Darwinian View of Life* (New York, Basic Books, 1995), p.133.

4 Haugen, G., *Good News About Injustice* (IVP, 1999), p.85.

5 Gen. 18.25.

6 Holland, T., *Dominion: The Making of the Western Mind* (Little, Brown, 2019), p.478.

7 Exod. 2.23–5.

8 The command to keep the Sabbath holy, for example, was referred to by Lord Justice Rix in *Copsey v WWB Devon Clays Ltd* (2005) as 'one of the earliest and closest to universally recognisable texts of employment law in favour of the employee of which we have knowledge'.

9 Prophets are called by God to call people back to true worship, which includes acting justly; see, for example, Amos 1–3.

10 Ps. 72.1–4 summarises the biblical teaching that kings are meant to bring justice and righteousness to the people they rule.

11 Italics added.

12 Hodge, C., *Conference Papers* (Wipt and Stock Publishers, 1879).

13 We're not sure of the exact original sermon, but here is a link to a similar one: https://www.monergism.com/thethreshold/articles/onsite/jesusourdefense.html

14 Heb. 7.25.

15 Luke 7.47.

7 To forgive us our sins

1 Lev. 16.21–2.

2 Bunyan, J., 'The Cross' (*The Pilgrim's Progress*, 1678), http://www.covenantofgrace.com/pilgrims_progress_loses_burden.htm. The idea for this illustration came from Mike Livingstone's helpful blog, *10 Things God Does With Our Sin*, https://goexplorethebible.com/blog/adults/10-things-god-does-with-our-sin-session-11-psalm-321-11.

3 Isa. 61.3.

4 Italics added.

5 Col. 2.14.

6 Thanks to Jared C. Wilson for this word and for his insights in this section.

7 Jer. 31.34; Isa. 43.25; Heb. 8.12, 10.17.

8 Mic. 7.19a.

9 Exod. 14.28.

10 We first came across this story in Philip Yancey's *Rumours of Another World* (Grand Rapids, MI, Zondervan, 2003), pp.223–4.

11 ten Boom, C., *The Hiding Place* (w. Sherrill, E., Sherrill, J.; Ada, MI, Chosen, 35th anniversary edn, 2006), p.310 (Scribd).

12 Open Doors supports the most persecuted religious group in the world, Christians, to courageously follow Jesus all over the world. We are big fans of the wonderful way they care for many like Jeovani. Check out their U.K. website: https://www.opendoorsuk.org

13 Open Doors Youth, 'CAR: Teenager Forgives His Attackers' (21 October 2019), https://opendoorsyouth.org/news/car-teenager-forgives-his-attackers.

8 And

1 Eph. 3.20.

2 Gen. 1.1.

3 Warren, K., 'Jeff Bezos Is the First Person Ever to Be Worth $200 Billion. This Is How the Amazon CEO's Immense Wealth Stacks Up to the Average US Worker, the British Monarchy, and Entire Countries' GDP' (*Insider*, 21 October 2020), https://www.businessinsider.com/how-rich-is-jeff-bezos-mind-blowing-facts-net-worth-2019-4?r=US&IR=T.

4 Gen. 3.1–4.

5 Thanks to Andrew Wilson's brilliant book *Spirit and Sacrament: An Invitation to Eucharismatic Worship* (Grand Rapids, MI, Zondervan, 2019), the second chapter of which inspired this section.

6 John 2.1–11.

7 Luke 5.1–11.

8 John 21.11.

9 Luke 9.10–17.

10 Mark 2.1–12.

11 Matt. 18.21–35.

12 Matt. 20.1–16.

13 Matt. 22.1–14.

14 Thank you to Kenneth Bailey for this powerful Middle Eastern cultural insight.

15 Luke 10.25–37.
16 Luke 15.11–32.
17 Matt. 5.39.
18 Matt. 5.40.
19 Matt. 5.41.
20 Matt. 5.43–8.
21 Wright, T., *Luke for Everyone* (SPCK, 2001), p.73.
22 John 3.16.
23 Eph. 1.3, italics added.
24 Tacitus was a Roman, hostile to Christianity.
25 Tacitus, *Annals*, 15.44.
26 Phil. 1.6.
27 Eph. 3.20.
28 You can watch the video here: https://www.youtube.com/watch
   /zIEIvi2MuEk

9 Cleanse us from all unrighteousness

1 We know that there is no indication that this man's leprosy
  is related to his sins. But we believe the Holy Spirit–inspired
  positioning of this miraculous story, after the Sermon on the
  Mount, connects it figuratively to *our* sin.
2 A better interpretation of 'blessed', according to Pennington, J.T.,
  *The Sermon on the Mount and Human Flourishing: A Theological
  Commentary* (Ada, MI, Baker Academic, 2017).
3 Thanks again to Tim Mackie for this insight; he was the first
  person to point this out to us.
4 Matt. 8.2 NIV.
5 1 John 3.20.
6 Our conclusion here leans heavily upon, amongst other scholars,
  Dr Craig Keener's excellent, exhaustive two-volume commentary
  on John's gospel, containing over 20,000 ancient extra-biblical
  references. Keener, C.S., *The Gospel of John: A Commentary*, vol. 1
  (Ada, MI, Baker Academic, 2012), pp.591–6.

7 Whilst she is not without sin, hers may not be as great as others',
particularly the men who are likely to have divorced her lightly, as
the culture then permitted, not to mention her current partner's
apparent refusal to legitimatise the relationship with marriage.

8 Gen. 24, 29; Exod. 2.15–21.

9 2 Kings 17.24–41.

10 Heb. 12.2.

11 Isa. 1.18.

12 Ezek. 36.25–7.

13 Ps. 51.2, 10.

14 Italics added.

15 'Rich Mullins: Pursuit of a Legacy'. Video (Nashville, TN, Reunion
Records, 1994). Quoted in Smith, J.B., *Rich Mullins: A Devotional
Biography – An Arrow Pointing to Heaven* (Scribd, 2000), p.217.

10 Application

1 2 Sam. 11.

2 1 Sam. 13.14; Acts 13.22.

3 Matt. 7.3.

4 Gen. 28.10–22.

5 Josh. 4.1–7.

6 Calvin and Battles, *Calvin*, p.634.

7 Piper, J., 'How Important Is It to Confess My Sin to Someone Other
Than God?' (desiringGod.org, 7 February 2018), https://www
.desiringgod.org/interviews/how-important-is-it-to-confess-my
-sin-to-someone-other-than-god.

8 Chester, T., *Truth We Can Touch: How Baptism and Communion
Shape Our Lives* (Wheaton, IL, Crossway, 2020), pp.44, 111.

Acknowledgements

We are, above all, thankful to our amazing triune God, without whom there is neither hope nor joy.

Massive thanks to our wonderful parents, who have been so good to us, alongside our supportive siblings. Thank you, fantastic children, for teaching us through your questions and for surprising us each day with new joys.

We are grateful to everyone who helped make this book possible: the wonderful people who shared their stories of forgiveness; Ian Matthews, Elizabeth Neep and the SPCK/Form publishing team; to Hannah Satterthwaite, Lianne De Vera, Tim Blaber, Andy Mehigan and Emily Brace for their edits; to John and Debby Wright for their gracious foreword, and the kind people who endorsed the book, especially in its early stages; to Stephen Sloan, who sparked the original preaching series idea; and to Emily Brace, Mike and Becci Tan and Luis and Lianne De Vera for their help publishing the book.

We owe a great deal of appreciation to Guy and Heather Miller, spiritual parents who have encouraged, supported and mentored us so well in recent years.

Thank you also to our Life Group at Westminster Chapel, who prayed this book onto the shelves.

Please accept our sincerest apologies if we have failed to acknowledge or reference you or anyone else appropriately. We have listened and read much over the years and can't always remember the original source of an idea or quote. We have tried our best to give credit appropriately in the endnotes.

Howard

I am indebted to the many gracious people who have invested in me, from those who shared the gospel with me at university – Kate Efomi (née West), Andy Grundy, Roger Carswell and others at Nottingham University Christian Union – to Christian leaders who took time to mentor me: Steve Sanderson, Martin Storey, David Shearman, Bob Campbell-Lamerton, Greg Haslam, Phil Varley, Andrew Lawrence, Malcolm Kayes and many from the Lawyers' Christian Fellowship. I am grateful to be part of two movements (Commission.Global and FIEC) and a church that are full of diverse, iron-sharpening-iron people, particularly the elders and the men of Westminster Chapel, who know me well and who continue to shape me for the better, alongside my best man Toby Bayliss and other key friends who know who they are. I am especially thankful to my amazing wife Holly, my best friend and greatest encourager.

Holly

Thank you to Eileen Milner, who brought me my first Bible in 1996, which started my curiosity about Jesus, and to the school friends who loved me enough to tell me about him. Thank you to Emily Aduah, who shaped me through my university years. Thank you to Gail McDonald, a wonderful email mentor. Thank you to Gillian Sloan – you have modelled a life of service and care – and Biola Akinyose for your willingness to pray with me each month. Thank you to Emma Lawrence for your word of knowledge that continues to give me the confidence to step out into new opportunities. Thank you to all my kind friends who have cheered and encouraged me. Lastly, thank you to my husband, Howard, for inviting me onboard this adventure. You are my encourager, mentor and best friend. You will always have my love.